Dear Father

A message of love
for priests.

D0017182

A new expanded edition of the popular classic by

Catherine Doherty

"*Dear Father* greatly expanded my appreciation for the priesthood. Catherine's immense love for the priesthood, coupled with her deep sense of how much the priest is called to imitate Christ in his sufferings and in his compassion for fallen humanity continue to challenge me. I am deeply indebted to her personally, for inspiring me to try to live this vocation as fully as I possibly can."

— Father Paul Burchat

"I have read your love letter, *Dear Father,* in one sitting. You know, my first mission as a newly ordained priest was hard. I really felt I had nothing. Complete emptiness. In the summer I asked to go on retreat, but there was no one to take my place. Next year, the same story. I was desperate but said, 'Lord, you are the source of your priest's life and strength. Give me what you think I need.' *Dear Father* was his answer!"

— a letter to Catherine from a priest in Africa

"I really loved *Dear Father*! Through the years I reflected on Catherine's loving and powerful message to Catholic priests, for whom she had a deep respect and love. I am anxious to share *Dear Father* with priests and future priests!"

— Bishop Paul V. Dudley

"I have given copies to various priests and all have commented on some aspect of the book which they felt was written especially for them. *Dear Father* says what most of us hesitate to say to our pastors—a message of affirmation and the guarantee of our prayers and understanding."

— Marikay Falby, *Prairie Messenger*

"Catherine gives me great consolation and a growing awareness of who a priest is. Every line in *Dear Father* touches me in chords that hear the eternal love of God."

— Father Gerry Wallner

"Catherine's love for the priesthood radiates through her writings. At the age of 12, she became aware of her calling to love priests and to pray for them. Her growing awareness of the powerful grace of priesthood and its clear identity in Christ are so necessary for priests and for the world today. In these days, we are acutely aware of the humanity of our priests, as indeed Catherine was; but her words suggest that she saw more deeply into the tremendous grace that is priesthood. I encourage everyone to read her book, especially priests."

— Father Stephen J. Rossetti, Ph.D., D.Min.
President, St. Luke Institute

Dear Father

A message of love for priests.

Catherine de Hueck Doherty

Edited by Father Patrick McNulty and Marian Heiberger

Madonna House Publications
2888 Dafoe Rd
Combermere ON K0J 1L0
www.madonnahouse.org/publications

Expanded Third Edition, 2001 (First published by Alba House, 1979)

Second printing, August 15, 2006 — feast of the Assumption

Printed in Canada

National Library of Canada Cataloguing in Publication Data

Doherty, Catherine de Hueck (née Kolyschkine), 1896–1985
        Dear Father : a message of love for priests.

Expanded 3rd ed.
ISBN 0-921440-76-6

        1. Catholic Church—Clergy. I. Title.

BX1912.D54 2001   253   C2001-904254-X

Title lettering by Marilyn Reaves
Design by Rob Huston

This book is set in Goudy, designed in 1915 by Frederic W. Goudy, one of the most popular and prolific American book and type designers.

To Father John T. Callahan

Founder of the priests of Madonna House

Foreword — 11
"What is a priest?"

I   **The call to priesthood — 17**
"Nothing can be greater in this world than a priest, nothing but God himself."

II   **Talk to us about God — 23**
"A priest is the reflection of God's love."

III   **Are priests relevant? — 31**
"A priest is a gift of God to man."

IV   **Holocausts of love — 37**
"The heart of a priest is a vessel of compassion… a chalice of love."

V   **Loneliness and priesthood — 45**
"A priest is a holy man because he walks before the face of the All-Holy."

VI   **Why we call you Father — 51**
"The heart of a priest is the trysting place of human and divine love."

VII   **You bring us joy — 61**
"A priest is a lover of God, a priest is a lover of men."

VIII   ***Alter Christus* - another Christ — 69**
"A priest is a symbol of the Word made flesh…"

IX   **Protect the Church — 77**
"The heart of a priest is pierced, like Christ's, with the lance of love."

X   **Anointed teachers — 89**
"A priest understands all things… forgives all things… encompasses all things."

XI   **A new vision of priesthood — 101**
"A priest is a man whose goal is to be another Christ… a man who lives to serve."

XII   **A life offered for priests — 111**
"A priest is a man who has crucified himself so that he too may be lifted up and draw all things to Christ."

XIII   **Our Lady, mother of priesthood — 119**
"Mary is my life. I hope I never have any other… she will lead me to her Son."

Anyone who knows Catherine Doherty would expect her to treat this subject just as she has done, frankly, directly, simply, lovingly. She portrays an exalted and innate idea of the Priesthood which characterizes any references she ever makes to it in all her writings. "Priest", she seems to say, "you are God-with-us, chosen by him to guide, and to show us how to love him and one another.

"Why should you be restless, dissatisfied, angry? Why look to other pastures? You have everything. Be what you are supposed to be—our friend, teacher, healer, servant. Be what Jesus wants you to be—another himself. Then your worries about identity will fade; you will find satisfaction and happiness; then you will no longer want to be other than you are; then you will be a bearer of peace and of hope to many confused people seeking guidance in today's doubt-filled world."

This message the author presents in an atmosphere of a profound love for priests, which can only flow from a love for the Eternal Priest and his chosen ones, a love that has grown over the years through prayer and penance. Her thrust is to encourage, to inspire, to protect, and to activate the priest as Christ's ambassador of love to all members of his flock, but especially to those who are yearning for their Lord.

✝ J.R. WINDLE
BISHOP OF PEMBROKE
MARCH 1, 1978

Foreword

"What is a priest?"

Many years ago, Catherine's husband Eddie received a letter in which he was asked: "What is a priest?" He puzzled over the question for some time and then went to see Catherine who was at her desk typing. "Someone has asked me," he said, "what a priest is. What would you say?" Without saying a word she picked up a pencil and wrote hastily on a piece of scrap paper the following:

> A priest is a lover of God,
> > a priest is a lover of men,
> > a priest is a holy man
> > because he walks before the face of the All-Holy.

> A priest understands all things,
> > a priest forgives all things,
> > a priest encompasses all things.

> The heart of a priest is pierced, like Christ's,
> > with the lance of love.

The heart of a priest is open, like Christ's,
    for the whole world to walk through.

The heart of a priest is a vessel of compassion,
    the heart of a priest is a chalice of love,
    the heart of a priest is the trysting place
    of human and divine love.

A priest is a man whose goal is to be another Christ;
    a priest is a man who lives to serve.

A priest is a man who has crucified himself
    so that he too may be lifted up
    and draw all things to Christ.

A priest is a man in love with God.

A priest is the gift of God to man
    and of man to God.

A priest is the symbol of the Word made flesh,
    a priest is the naked sword of God's justice,
    a priest is the hand of God's mercy,
    a priest is the reflection of God's love.

Nothing can be greater in this world than a priest,
    nothing but God himself.

When I first came across this poem, this mystical musing of Catherine Doherty's, I did not like it at all; I considered it a nice poem by a nice lady who obviously had some unique, even romantic sense of the priesthood, but it did not seem to apply to me. Or rather, it was outside of my grasp as priest.

I would not be surprised if some of you would also have an unfavorable reaction to this "poem" on many counts. Not the least of which is your sense that even if the poem represents some truth it is not your experience of being priest; it is not who you see yourself to be or perhaps even who you want to be. But I would also not be surprised if most of you are touched by it in a way which you cannot quite verbalize or understand at first.

Yet I now realize that from the time I first read it in the 70's, indeed from the time I first met Catherine in the 60's to this very day, being priest has been the gradual and mysterious unfolding of the depths of this poem in my heart and my life whether I wanted it or not at the time.

I believe that is what happened to most priests who knew Catherine personally and what happens to those now who know her only through her writings. She truly did have an incredible, indeed mystical, sense of Christ's priesthood and thus of those ordained to that priesthood. As she poured over us the healing balm of her heroic love and compassion which flowed from her suffering for us, she was not afraid to speak to us the "prophetic" and powerful truth about ourselves.

I first met Catherine Doherty in the parking lot of Madonna House in 1964. I was getting out of my car when she came up to me, took my hand, kissed it and said, "Welcome, Father, it is a privilege for us to have you here." Well, I did not want to be called, "Father"—I was one of those modern priests of the 60's, and I did not want to be considered a "privilege," as if I were someone or something special. I left as soon as I could.

I did cautiously return to Madonna House for very short-term visits a few more times and also had some intense correspondence with Catherine by mail for about four years. Then in 1968 my priestly world fell apart and I was seriously thinking of leaving the priesthood and the Church. Because I didn't have any place else to go at the time I returned to Madonna House. It was only then I began to learn the secret of why she kissed our hands and called us, "Father."

We may not seem to ourselves to be a priest like Catherine envisions in her poem but this mysterious woman of God has touched that "priestly place" in thousands of priestly hearts all over the world. Whenever I re-read this book I know once again the healing power of her heroic faith in the priesthood of Jesus Christ and of her words of compassion and hope to those of us ordained to it.

Sometimes even she did not understand how or why her words were so powerful, and it puzzled her. In 1981, four years before her death, on the occasion of her trip to Rome for a private audience and Mass with Pope John Paul II and a whirlwind speaking tour in Paris where she was already well known for her book *Poustinia*, she writes,

> ...Why is Christ sending me? Well, the answer comes very simply: "Catherine, I am sending you to preach the Gospel because your words are words of fire. Perhaps you shall never know how your words are fire to listeners. You preach the Gospel with your whole being. That is what I need..."

And then she says,

> I'm simply trying to explain to you, whoever will listen to this, who God is to me; what joy, what infinite joy, seems to grow out of his pain and mine. Joy!
>
> I ask him, "Lord, bless me on this venture. You're here, you're near. Bless me." And he has. Can you imagine? In a little *isba* (cabin) at the end of nowhere in the little village of Combermere, God blessed me. Alleluia! Alleluia! Alleluia!"

Yes, my dear friend Catherine, God blessed you and blessed all priests through you. Alleluia! Alleluia! Alleluia!

FATHER PATRICK MCNULTY,
staff priest of Madonna House,
editor of the expanded edition.

I | The call to priesthood

"Nothing can be greater in this world than a priest, nothing but God himself."

The year is 1951. In North America the future seemed bright and the Church in very good shape; vocations to the priesthood were more than plentiful. In that year Father Rawley Myers, a diocesan priest and director of vocations, edited a book entitled, The Greatest Calling*. Subtitled,* A Presentation of the Priesthood by Famous Catholics, *the book was 183 pages of North American witness in answer to the question, "What is the priesthood?"*

The articles were written by bishops, priests, nuns, a father of a family, a football player, a teacher and an editor—famous folk such as Bishop Fulton Sheen, Clare Booth Luce, Father Patrick Peyton, Frank Leahey, Father Daniel Lord and a special chapter by Emmanuel Cardinal Suhard. Lo and behold, on page 103 begins a five page article by a rather unknown lay woman, Catherine Doherty.

In 1951 Madonna House was only five years old. The Friendship House movement for which Catherine had poured out her life was petering out. And though the major tragedies involving clergy in Catherine's apostolic life were in the past, they were still fresh in her memory. But she was already speaking of the priesthood in somewhat mystical terms.

---

* *The Greatest Calling*, ed. Father Rawley Myers (McMullen, 1951)

Catherine's article stands out like a thorn among the roses. One would have to read the book to see that hers is the only one which explains the great crucifixion which was about to come upon the priesthood all over the world. Catherine not only believed that such a crucifixion belonged to the heart of the mystery of the priesthood but she had already suffered it herself.

Her article is written in the form of a letter.

Dear Friend,

You have asked me to tell you something about the great vocation of the priesthood, because you think you have a call to it, but you are not quite sure and so you want some light on the matter, from me.

I feel honored at your request. I know, too, why you are asking me, an ordinary lay woman, to help you, for I remember telling you some time ago of my great love for priests, and of the need this tragic world has for them.

So I will try to tell you what is in my heart about this stupendous vocation. But I will not, for I cannot, go over ground already covered. Nor can I wax sentimentally pious about its glories. For one does not go sentimental over a stark cross and a Man crucified to it!

To be a priest is to be indeed called by God, for he says clearly, "I have chosen you; you have not chosen me." It is also to be the son of God, for he said, "Thou art my son" and "Thou art a priest forever in the line of Melchisedech."

Do you know what that means? It means that you will be all his, but that your life will be the loneliest lived on this earth, naturally speaking; that you will walk shrouded in loneliness, amidst multitudes.

You will indeed have to "arise, sell what you possess, and follow Christ." (Mt 19:21) Do you understand now, in the flower of your youth, what you are asked to do, to be? Slowly, your life will pattern itself on his. You will walk wearily amidst people, night and day, bringing them the glad tidings of love. Yet they will laugh in your face and go their way. Your garments will be dusty from days spent in the search for souls. Eventide will come and your hands will be empty of them, and your face covered with the spittle of their derision and refusals.

You will deal in sin all your life. You will know and comprehend better than others, the enormity of just one mortal sin. You will have to steel yourself to face rivers of it, seas of it. It will choke you, engulf you, make you tremble and weak.

You will wear the most beautiful garments devised by the ingenuity of men, several times a day, maybe. You will move amongst gold and incense brought from distant places. But you will have to be poor, even as the Prisoner of Love whom you serve in the tabernacle is poor.

You will have to be poor in worldly goods—to defeat the modern idolatry of material possessions. You will have to be poor in spirit and poor in will, for you will have surrendered yours to your bishop; poor in person and in consolations. In fact, a time will come when you, like your Master, will have to be naked poor; you will follow a naked Christ unto his Cross.

And you will be crucified, too, by the flesh that will still be with you; by the devil who will not let you be; by the lukewarm and indifferent amongst your flock; by the rich and greedy in your front pews; by the unbelievers and the scoffers outside; and by your own weakness and fears.

Then you will be as one dead—a piece of clay—for the Master Sculptor to work his masterpiece in you. You will feel the touch of his divine fingers, pounding, molding, hurting the clay that is you. It will be God the Father making you unto the likeness of his Son, the Man of Sorrows.

You will know darkness as few people know it. It will be a palpable, touchable, heavy darkness, that will encompass you on all sides. There will be nary a pinpoint of light in it, and at times it may almost suffocate you. You will have to keep on walking, living, having your being in that darkness, perhaps for the span of your whole natural life. You will have to walk in it by the light of your faith only. And what is more, while your soul is steeped in this utter darkness you yourself will have to be a light to a thousand feet.

Doubts and fears, temptations and even sin, will try to walk with you. Often you will be misunderstood by those above you, and those below. There will be some who will want to use you as a tool of their own design. Others will stone you with ridicule. And through all this you seemingly will be alone.

But that is not all. In our day and time, you will have to be ready at a moment's notice, and maybe without any, to lay down your life for your God and your flock. And what is perhaps more terrible, you may be deprived of this flock and of your Church, and may not even be allowed to die like a man, but perhaps be made to live in the dungeon of a prison or in a forced-labour concentration camp.

Are you ready?

If you are, then yours will be the most glorious life ever lived. You will be Christ's envoy, for it is said, "Behold I establish thee a minister and a witness." You will become a living symbol of God, not merely by your words, but by your entire life. And in your flesh the infinite and joyous folly of the Cross will be realized.

At your word sinners will rise from the death of sin and shed their ghostly wrappings and, who knows, become great saints of God and his love.

In truth you will bring, not peace but a sword. You will be a sign of contradiction that will make men think and live. You will be a minister of fire, ordained to spread that fire on the earth. You will also be a minister of restlessness, the dispenser of a new hunger and thirst.

You will be poor, and your poverty will enrich millions. You will be chaste with the chastity of an immense and burning love for a God who has reserved it for himself—from a few specially consecrated sons. Your chastity will heal lust in many hearts, and will give you the power to command its demons out of many parts of the world. For you will make your own the words, *Deus meus et omnia* (my God and my all).

True, you will walk in darkness, perhaps for your entire life, perhaps for a few years of it, or days. But at the same time you will be a light that will kill the tragic, evil darkness men face in our dark days of atheism and secularism.

Loneliness will be your constant companion. Yet your presence will be a blessing to all, and will disperse loneliness in others. You will deal in sin all your life but it will not touch you, for you will walk in the glory of the Lord, whom your hands touch daily, whom your words bring down to us.

You will be hungry with many hungers but you will fill souls and hearts with the Bread of Life. You will slaken the infinite thirst of men for God, with the living waters of Truth.

You will pray, and heaven will listen, hell tremble, and death hear.

At your word, a child of sin will become a child of God. A youth will become a soldier of Christ, a sinner a saint. Hungry men will be filled, dying ones sped homeward in peace.

You will open your mouth and teach, and the fullness of Truth will come out of it. The Word will take flesh again and walk amongst men, and many shall arise and follow him.

Your hands will heal, and bless, and help. Your presence will bring joy and peace. You yourself will walk in peace, and be an artisan of its lasting city. You will know much, and be humble. You will pray much and then pray again. For you will know that prayer is your strength, and that of your flock. You will fast and do penance, and you will be a vessel filled to the brim; many will come to drink from these hallowed waters.

You will walk apart, and multitudes will follow you wherever you go—even into the desert. Because they are in your shadow, the desert will bloom.

You will be all things to all men. You, like Christ, will be lifted up, for men to see and follow you. But you will not mind being crucified naked on a Cross, because Christ will be on the other side, and you will be lost in the ecstasy of being with him, of being his own.

All this you will be, and all these things will happen to you, if you arise now and answer the mere whisper that your young soul hears, and that you are not quite sure about.

Yes, my dear young friend, that is what it means to be a priest. That is the vocation to the priesthood as I see it. Humbly, reverently, I pass on my vision of it to you, for when all is said and done, the call you hear is the call to be another Christ, an *alter Christus*.

Can there be a greater miracle of God's grace? Can there be a greater vocation? If there is I do not know about it.

II | Talk to us about God

"A priest is the reflection of God's love."

People's hunger for God is rising like a tide that nothing can stem; a response must be forthcoming. Either we answer or someone else will. People are seeking God everywhere; youth still travels across continents looking for him.

As people travel far and wide to find God, their hunger meets fear. Strangely enough, the fear is in the men who have been touched by God in a very special way, in the tremendous sacrament of the priesthood. Yet it is to them that we laity look, imploring and beseeching them for answers. We feel we have to have someone "give us God." By this we mean giving us the Word of God.

How does a man, a person, give God to another? Let us look for a moment at the fear of the men of God. In their own minds they seem to have lost face. They are looking for their identity. They are seeking what they call community. But do they seek the Alpha and Omega? The first community that we Christians, especially the men of God, should be one with, is the Holy Trinity—the immense and incomprehensible, mysterious, awesome, compassionate community of the Most Holy Trinity.

Once we enter into the fire and flame of this community then, as Christ said, we shall perform miracles as great as he has, and greater. One of the great miracles that a human being can perform is to preach the word of God. The man who preaches the Word of God is a miracle of God's grace because he doesn't do the preaching, God does. His first step is to be one with God, to be of one mind and heart with him.

What do we hunger for? Explanations of theological or doctrinal matters or the Catechism? No. We hunger to be taught, to be led, and to be healed by the Word of God, by love. Teach us how to love. Teach us true knowledge. Teach us how to pray. Do not satisfy just our intellects. Teach us not only about God but how to *know* God himself. He is not exactly found in books, except one Book.

God reveals himself to those who love him with an open heart, to those who listen to his words which come to us, now like the whisper of a spring breeze, now in a terrible storm which tears us apart.

Don't be afraid. Don't seek your "identity." You have it. You are a man touched by God, and we the laity know it. We love you, even if some are hostile to you and castigate you, because they think that certain of you have let us down. But don't be afraid. You have been touched by God, and so it is not you who speaks, but he. Let us hear his voice and, because you allowed him to speak through you, we shall know him.

But how is this going to happen if you are looking for your identity all over the place? If you are so busy seeking a community? If you are thinking of interpersonal relations?

I cannot understand what interpersonal relations are unless I first have a very deep interpersonal relation with the Most Holy Trinity, and especially with Jesus Christ, my Brother, and with Mary, my Mother. When you love someone you have an interpersonal relation. Priests are called to love thousands of people. With each person you are to have the interpersonal relation of a man who leads other persons to God. That is interpersonal enough!

We speak much of community these days. You are a member of the people of God; you are in a community. The community loves you and expects from you not eloquence but that "something else" which is more than mere polish of words and of sermons prepared three days in advance. We hope for words that come from your heart because you have listened to his heart. Then we know that he speaks through you.

I think now of a Man sitting on a green mountain, talking to people who couldn't read or write, mostly cooks and slaves and uneducated people. The educated ones didn't sit on the grass. They may have stood apart but they didn't listen because they didn't have ears to hear. We the laity have a heart that is hungry for God. Give us that knowledge of God which came to you when you were alone with him in his immense silence.

If you ask a Russian what prayer is, he will say, "To stand still before God so that you can talk to men." Give us that knowledge. I do not care if you stutter. I couldn't care less if you are a little afraid. Who wouldn't be afraid to stand there in faith, in a darkness that surpasses all understanding, and open his mouth. But God said, "Open your mouth and I will fill it." A little fear is the beginning of wisdom.

Teach us God, after you have met him in prayer and in the study of the Word. The Word is like a tremendous, mysterious teacher. You might be a Scripture scholar, familiar with every passage, but if you read it on your knees the light of the Holy Spirit will fall on a word and it will open itself before you like a flower or a nut cracked by an immense nutcracker.

Teach us how to know God because you know him. Teach us how to pray because you are men of prayer. We shall know if you are or not; you do not have to tell us. For we are your flock and you the shepherds, and we know your voice; we know you because we are children, in a way—and Christ told us that he loves children.

Don't pay attention to our present sophistication. We might be a Ph.D., we might be a lay theologian, but when you tell us parables like he did then we shall know the Truth, and the Truth will set us free. And you will be free because in telling parables you disappear and he appears. Tell us stories as he did, the simpler the better.

Your very insecurity will become a grace to turn to him rather than to a thousand psychological, psychiatric and other remedies. Nothing wrong with these, but in proper proportion. They will not answer the hunger in your own heart, for your hearts are hungry to give us God just as our hearts are hungry to receive him. You know deep down in your soul that that is why you were touched by God: to give us God.

Is love an emotion? Is love a state? Or is it a person? It is the person of a Carpenter who spent thirty years in a village of no account just making tables and chairs for the villagers. There were three years of preaching, which at the time did not make much impression on the powerful, and not too much impact on the middleclass. He preached. His voice and word were like a seed in the wind. The megaphone of the centuries carried him into the world, and still does and always will.

What is love? Some say you have to be married to know love. I have been married twice. Do I know love? Well, I know the ecstasy of the flesh, indeed I do, but one Communion, one reception of the Body and Blood of the Lord is ecstasy beyond understanding. The penetration of this tremendous Lover into my being leaves everything else pale!

Teach us how to love a person, because love is a Person. Until I, through your person and through the Word that you share with me, have met him who is the source of all love, I shall not know what love is, celibate or married. Reveal the Lord to us from your knowledge of him and your understanding of who you are. Do not be afraid to tell us what is in your heart.

You are so unsure today, insecure somehow, and in a way, so frightened. Remember that Christ says, "Where two or three are gathered in my name, there I am." He is here and everywhere. And as St. Paul says, "I live not, Christ lives in me." That unity with God is what we are hungry for. We don't care if you are fat or thin, good looking or not. We don't care about that. Teach us about God.

I have so little to offer you except a tremendous love for the priesthood. The laity today are rambunctious. They go around scratching you here and putting a knife in your back there, or they may seem to. Well, I would like to come with the oils of my love and the wine of my compassion to heal your wounds, for I know some of them are deep. But even then be joyful. Look at what the laity of his time, the priests of his time, the whole setup of his time, did to Christ.

Today the bishops are still our whipping posts—less than before, but still whipping posts. Priests and laity, all of us, are trying to hit someone else. Why? Even the pope does not escape this ire. Where is charity? How can you preach it when there is no charity in all these discussions? Please don't be pacifists who go around trying to stop a war on the one hand while hitting their own brothers with the other. Let us begin at the beginning.

How can you preach the Word of God, and how can I or anyone else listen, if our hearts are full of anger against the bishop or another priest, or against another lay person? Before you partake of the Holy Species, go and make peace with your neighbour; otherwise you blaspheme the Body and Blood of Christ.

I wish you could hear the laity who love you and the bishops and the pope. Why don't you rest in our love? The Father, Son and Holy Spirit dwell in our hearts. Preach the Word of God to us. Make it short. Make it simple. Talk to us about our hunger and your hunger and tell us that he who speaks through you can heal us and assuage this hunger. We will respond and come to you because you are Christ, especially when you preach the Word, his word. You can heal us and you can assuage our hunger. Eloquence is not important. Sincerity is, and truth is.

It's perhaps foolish of me to say that the clergy needs prayer above all else. Stand still before God so you can speak to us. Open your heart to him and you will be preachers whom children will follow on the street.

You are a priest; don't try to be something else that you think may be easier. Give us God and we shall go into the ghettoes; we shall clean them. We shall love. We shall work. We shall pray, because you have taught us how. Yes, you have shown us how because you have seen and felt and touched who you are and who he is. Because of that we will have touched and known and fallen in love with him who is love. You will send us forth like a thousand sparks of fire of the Holy Spirit.

There is only one way to come to us and for us to come to you, and that is through his cross which stands forever bathed in a light that is almost blinding.

We are living in the resurrected Christ, not in the dead One. Christ is in our midst now and forever. Give us that light! Give us that joy! Give him to us and your identity crisis will be solved and you will have the community of the Most Holy Trinity of which you are a part.

There is a song of silence that man hears coming from the heart of other men. It is so simple, my dearly beloved Fathers, to fall in love with God, to be one with this great community of the Most Holy Trinity. Stand still before him so that you can speak to others, since God has spoken to you. Then together we shall renew the face of the earth. Love is the only thing that can do it in this time of hate, strife and misery. Love speaks all languages. It is simple and humble.

The one and only priesthood of Christ is so powerful. I, a member of his Mystical Body and one of your flock, say to you today, when the Church lies almost prone, her garments seemingly torn, I say to you: Teach us to understand. Teach us to pray. Teach us how to love. You will know, because you love and you pray; and because you are one with him. Speak to us then in any way you wish, because he will be speaking through you. Remember to let him.

I pray without ceasing for you, for in my poverty I can do nothing else. I beg you, start with Christ and all the rest shall be added to you.

III

Are priests relevant?

"A priest is the gift of God to man."

I remember the day when there were no priests in Petrograd. In the early days of the Revolution, when things were so unsettled, priests were shot on sight, as were many other people. Jewish rabbis, Protestant ministers, Orthodox priests, all were shot or disposed of in some way.

Alone, a tiny parish was still surviving, and those of us who knew about it participated in the Mass in the middle of the night. One night when the priest had just consecrated the Bread, the door opened, a rifle was thrust through, a shot was fired, and the priest fell dead. The consecrated Bread fell onto the floor. Two soldiers came up then, ground it under their heels, and turning to us said, "Where is your God? Under our heel!"

An old man answered, "Lord, forgive them, even if they know what they do." Shamed or embarrassed, the two soldiers left the church. The old man gave us Communion with the remnants of the Body of Christ. We buried the priest.

And then there was none! No one to hear one's confession and give absolution. No one to give us Viaticum and the last rites, as they were called then. No one to offer Mass. Anyone who has gone through this tragedy knows what it means to be without a priest. I never thought I would live to see the day when parishes would be closed and monasteries sold for lack of vocations, and departures.

So when I see in the news questions such as, "Are priests relevant to our modern world?" they leave me numb and I cry silently out of the very depths of my soul. I beg Christ to touch, with the "spittle" of his grace (Mk 7:33), the eyes and ears of those who ask such questions, so that they may cease to "have ears and hear not, have eyes and see not," so that they may become witnesses and believers.

I went to the Bible to pray for this intention, to the Acts of the Apostles, chapter six, entitled, *Earliest Missions:*

> About this time when the number of disciples was increasing, the Hellenists made a complaint against the Hebrews; in the daily distribution, their own widows were being overlooked. So the twelve called a full meeting of the disciples and addressed them: "It would not be right for us to neglect the word of God so as to give out food. You, brothers, must select from among yourselves seven men of good reputation, filled with the Spirit and with wisdom; we will hand over this duty to them and continue to devote ourselves to prayer and the service of the word."

It went on to say that the assembly approved, and seven men were chosen. (I believe some women were chosen also, and that deacons and deaconesses did this work.) The Book of Acts goes on to say that the word of the Lord continued to spread, the number of disciples in Jerusalem was greatly increased, and a large group of priests made their submission to the faith.

How then can a questionnaire ask if priests are relevant to this secularized, pluralistic, permissive, upside-down world in which we live?

Greece and Rome, Alexandria and Antioch, and other major cities of that day were very much like big cities in our own era. True, they worshiped pagan gods, but certainly they were secular and more than permissive. Slavery existed and made life easy for the free citizens of the world. Sexual perversions played a large part, with all that means for a society.

Yet that began to be changed through twelve ordinary men who were very unlearned, who had the strangest training that was ever given to priests: they were in the company of God for about three years. These men seemed totally unconcerned about the relevancy of their calling.

They knew they were relevant. They knew their role. They knew their identity. It was all wrapped up in the deep understanding that they were to preach the Good News. That, and that only, was their job. They knew they were to do this and to offer the Eucharistic Sacrifice. They had been trained by the Lord himself who had formed them and given them the Spirit of Wisdom to know their identity in the Church.

Are priests relevant to our modern world? The question continues to shake me to the very essence of my being. I, a pilgrim of the Lord, have been traveling across our vast North American continent, spending my life in its Harlems, its slums, its poverty-stricken rural areas, among its hippies and its beatniks, always surrounded by youth, always surrounded by priests and young men studying to be priests. I have lectured over and over again, but I have also listened. Everywhere I have listened. To my desk come some 28,000 letters a year. And what is the result of all this listening and talking?

There is a pain which surpasses almost all other pain: that of watching a priest forget who he is. It is the pain of not being heard when we cry out to him, "Look, we don't want you to be a psychiatrist. We don't want you to be a great theologian."

You have an identity; you have a role. As long as you are looking for them we will be left in the desert under the hot sun with no water, and there will be no manna. True, God will come himself and he will console us, but he will weep over you. For you, like St. John the Baptist, "must decrease," and yet you must also increase, in Christ, while he himself increases in you.

It is time, especially in this culture, that we cease trying to prove something. A priest wants to prove that he is useful. He wants to be relevant, productive. He uses so many words that really don't mean a thing, that pass into one of our lay ears and out the other. For a while we listen and say, "Yes," and then, through prayer or even without conscious prayer, people begin to feel that something is wrong. What is it? What is wrong?

It is only because the answer is so simple that I permit myself to give a few facts about myself, to show that I know with a knowledge that no one can take from me, that if there is one relevant person today in this world it is a priest.

The world is hungry for the Good News of the Lord. The world is hungry for truth, for love, for a meaning in life, for hope, for faith, for charity. The world is hungry for food—the food of the Eucharist. Aye, it is hungry for more than bread, which indeed, this world needs too, the ordinary, daily bread to assuage the hunger of millions. Nevertheless, I repeat, from deep and exceedingly painful experience, the world is more hungry for truth, for God, for his Good News, than it is even for the bread of daily life.

The priests of today must somehow gather together as did the Twelve: "So the Twelve called a full meeting." What did they say at this meeting of the disciples and the people of God? "It would not be right for us to neglect the word of God so as to give out food."

When this word from Scripture enters deeply into the hearts of modern priests, they will know how relevant they are. The Twelve went on to say: "We will hand over this duty to them [the laity] and continue to devote ourselves to prayer and to the service of the word."

Oh, if only priests preached the Word on the corners of streets, on the strange, modern forums: little squares where the hobo and prostitute rest on a hot day in our big cities. If only they preached the Word in cocktail lounges and cafes where society still floats around aimlessly. If only they preached the Word in ghettos and on the main streets of cities, towns, and villages of our vast land. If only they preached it while traveling in the night, hitch-hiking with truck drivers, riding in boats that might be wrecked by a storm, being present in factories during lunch hour, as well as in churches.

If priests would pray for the courage to do such preaching of the Good News, if they really devoted their time to the service of the Word, there would be no question of their relevancy! Crowds would follow them, and their identity would truly be revealed to them, for the Son of Truth would illuminate them all.

In all the words printed about priests, little is mentioned about prayer or the service of the Word. Much is being said about "feeding the widows," which in our modern times has a thousand connotations.

No one is more relevant than a priest who understands his role as the servant of the Word, as the man who can give us God under the form of bread and wine. Then we, the laity, may be filled with the wisdom we need in order to love and serve our fellow man, as did the deacons and deaconesses of the early Church.

I pray, "Lord, that the eyes of all your priests may be opened to the truth, that their ears may be opened to hear where their real relevancy lies. They are relevant because they are You."

IV | Holocausts of love

*"The heart of a priest is a vessel of compassion...
a chalice of love."*

You are a sign of love, as well as of joy and hope. St. Paul has the best definition of love that I have encountered. He begins very simply by talking about the order of importance in spiritual gifts. Coming to love he says, "Be ambitious for the higher gifts. And I am going to show you a way that is better than any of them." St. Paul removes from love all that is not of God, purifies it and makes it holy. He lifts it up.

"If I have all the eloquence of men or of angels, but speak without love, I am simply a gong booming or a cymbal clashing." How often has this been true of Christians. How often has it been true of you, beloved Fathers? Rounded out phrases, beautiful sermons given with eloquence. Why is it that people did not rush to you, did not thank you, did not surround you as they would have surrounded Christ? They politely passed by you saying, "Charming sermon, Father. Very nice," but walked away rather sorrowful. Why?

"If I have the gift of prophecy, understanding all the mysteries there are, and knowing everything, and if I have faith in all its fullness, to move mountains, but without love, then I am nothing at all." Can you imagine yourself possessing the gift of healing, the gift of prophecy, the gift of discernment, plus, of course, the seven gifts of the Holy Spirit? But if you exercise

them without love as St. Paul says, "...then I am nothing at
all."

Those words are frightening, aren't they, since a lot of us
exercise the gifts of the Holy Spirit because they put us in the
limelight. They add to our self-glorification. It's most tragic
when, given all these gifts to bring others to God, we hug them
to ourselves, in a sense, and take a certain pride in possessing
them. Of course St. Paul is right: then we are nothing.

"If I give away all that I possess, piece by piece, and if I
even let them take my body to burn it, but am without love, it
will do me no good whatever." Those are very strong words,
aren't they, beloved Fathers?

Love, or "charity" as St. Paul calls it, is, in all gradations,
the very essence of your being, since when you possess God,
you possess Love. Ordained in his ministry—but even more,
ordained in him because he is you and you are him—the one
thing you have to give is love.

You must give it away abundantly. You can plunge every
hour, every minute, every second, into the fathomless, bottomless love of Christ. You must give away the love that God
gave us, the love that he exhibited in his incarnation, passion
and crucifixion. It's yours. Yours, to have and to hold for a second! Just for a second, then to give away lavishly. It will come
back to you from the very Source from which it came when
you were first ordained. So love is what you have to give all the
time.

But let's look further. "Love is always patient and kind." I
think of the sixties: the gleeful unkindness of so many carica-
tures of the hierarchy, the pope; making fun of things that are
not funny. The sacred cannot be reduced to the profane. Not
at any time.

"Love is always patient and kind." Can I examine my con-
science and say that I am patient and kind to authority, to my
brethren, to those so-called "beneath me," to the poor, to the

humble, to everybody? And yet, my dearly beloved Fathers, God is patient with you, infinitely patient. You may push and pull and explain him away in your theologies, or want to eradicate him, in other theologies. Why? Has the source of love dried up? All you have to do is turn your face to God and ask for love, since God is merciful, and no matter how much you have hurt him he will immediately restore communication between you and him.

"Love is never rude or selfish; never vulgar." Yet the way we have been treating the whole set-up of the Church is really tragic, isn't it? And while we did it, guilt came over us. We laughed, didn't we? We thought we were relevant because we joined the group of people who laughed. But did you notice that those groups wept while they laughed? Did you see their tears? They were hidden in their hearts, but you, with the gift of discernment, could have given peace to those who laughed at God and at his ministers. God is not mocked, but so many didn't remember that.

"Love takes no pleasure in other people's sins but delights in the truth; it is always ready to excuse, to trust, to hope, and to endure whatever comes." Just read that again, because it's so important. "Love takes no pleasure in other people's sins." It never points a finger at another, only at oneself. Love naturally delights in the truth because it not only speaks it and thinks it, but knows itself so well and knows that God is always ready to forgive.

You often see the prodigal son returning to the Father, and in confession you, in Jesus' name, excuse and annihilate any confessed fault. *Ego te absolvo...* It's not you who is absolving. It's God, but through you his pardon comes again and again. If it comes to your penitents, how about you being a penitent at Christ's feet? I am sure you are because love is like that. It goes there often.

"Love hopes and trusts and endures whatever comes." Of course it trusts. Above all, it trusts the untrustworthy for the simple reason that you and I are being trusted. We are very untrustworthy, don't you think so, dear Fathers? With all the blessings, with all the miracles of our being, we are still untrustworthy, aren't we? So if God trusts us we have to trust the other, especially the untrustworthy.

Not for us the saying, "Oh, I have just given this chap a dollar and now he is back again with the same excuse." Christ said, "If someone asks you for a coat, give your tunic also." Those who receive it have nobody but you. True, they might go and sell it for a couple of bucks to get a drink, but by now everybody knows that drinking is a disease. You are not going to refuses a sick man a cloak, are you?

St. Paul goes on to tell us that even if I deliver my body to be burned, but have no love, I am like a gong ringing in an emptiness that is not filled with God. Love makes the slightest gesture beautiful and holy. The sharing of a match. The sharing of oneself. The opening of oneself to another. The sharing of a room. The sharing of money with love. All become part of Christ's act. Now you are like Christ, and no one knows what happened to the man to whom you gave that cloak, that dollar or that match. No, nobody knows.

It's rather obvious, isn't it, that the one thing God asks from us, whether we be laity, priests, pope, beggar or prostitute, is to love one another, because through loving one another we love him. That is the quality of love that should interest a priest above all else.

St. Paul continues: "But if there are gifts of prophecy, the time will come when they must fail; or the gift of languages, it will not continue forever; and knowledge—for this, too, the time will come when it must fail. For our knowledge is imperfect and our prophesying is imperfect; but once perfection comes, all imperfect things will disappear. When I was a child,

I used to talk like a child...Now all childish ways are put behind me. Now we are seeing a dim reflection in a mirror; then we shall be seeing face to face. The knowledge that I have now is imperfect; but then I shall know as fully as I am known."

All gifts of the Holy Spirit will cease. Love alone will remain. You will appear before God, I hope, in a cloak of love. It will be smooth and red and beautiful, reflecting the sun.

Your priestly life is a life of love, dearly beloved Fathers, and this kind of love that I am talking about now, the one described by St. Paul, deals easily with earthly love. It deals easily with it because you have tasted the love of the Father. You have been immersed in that sea of love that is your ordination. That is the secret of chastity, my friends. The ability to love as Christ loves: that is the secret of chastity.

Remember this when temptations against Love come to you, because that's what they are: temptations against the incredible Love in which you were immersed by the sacrament of your ordination. You can understand the vow of chastity only in that context. Without it there can be no vow of chastity.

You are covered with the crimson cloak of God's love. It is crimson because he died for you and me, but especially for you, in a manner of speaking. You are clothed with it, for it is like your other skin. You can walk in peace the road that is laid out for you by God. That strange peace comes to a priest, I imagine, when he contemplates what the sacrament of the priesthood has given him.

Yes, you are a sign of hope wherever you go, but you lift men up to heights unknown when you are chaste. They truly begin to understand what holiness is, and after all, why have we all been baptized in the death and resurrection of Christ? To become holy. We all should be holy, looking at our Head, but especially you, walking in the crimson cloak given to you by Christ at your ordination as a young man. Now we can touch the crimson cloak; we too can be chaste, according to our state of life. We too can consider chastity which we have thrown away as if it were an old rag. Your chastity, Fathers, and that of others, is the warp and woof of holiness.

While thinking about chastity and love I received two other words that seem to supersede chastity and love. The words were compassion and mercy, and I realized that they, of course, stemmed from love. I began to meditate about these beautiful virtues.

To me a virtue is an outpouring of a heart. Do you think that is theologically correct, to call a virtue an outpouring of a heart?

I must admit that compassion and mercy are very much entwined in my heart, like Siamese twins. When I think of compassion and mercy, I automatically think of God, because isn't he the All-Merciful One, the All-Compassionate One?

I discovered something new: I did not know that the human heart can hold a sea of compassion. A brook, a little river maybe. But a sea? No! No, I did not know that the human heart could contain a sea of compassion and of mercy. But I recently found that mine can.

One night when I was praying I suddenly saw one wall of my log cabin vanish—I must have dozed off. Anyhow, it had gone, and my not overly big dwelling was filled with priests. Priests filled with doubts. Priests filled with pain, a hidden pain. Priests who were waiting to be laicized. Priests who wanted to marry. Priests who were thinking of divorce. Priests who were staying where they were appointed to stay but looking so very tired. Some of them were positively exhausted.

From my mind and heart and soul there vanished every desire to accuse any of those priests for their lack of faith, their weakness or immaturity. I was suddenly filled with love and compassion. I wanted to take them in my arms as if I were their mother or their older sister. I wanted to console them. I wanted to tell them how much I loved their priesthood which is the one priesthood of Christ. I wanted to tell them how I and all of us, the laity, need them. But even our needs disappeared in this love and compassion that engulfed me.

I wish I could speak, write, or somehow convey to every priest who is in the throes of doubts, pain, inner battles and weariness, that he is not alone. That in the rural depths of Canada there is one woman who loves the priesthood with a love that she cannot understand herself, for it transcends her understanding; but her heart is a sea of love and compassion!

I wish I could write and tell every priest that I share his pain, whatever pain it might be, because I love the priesthood. You are my brothers and my Fathers and you are so lonely and so lost these days. But I cannot write to every priest. I simply say again that the doors of Madonna House are wide open. We have a humble, simple house for priests. We have *poustinias*, log cabins where one can be alone with God and rest and can perhaps relearn to pray, if this be a need.

Priests are men twice set apart by the Lord. You've heard the Lord speak twice, once at Baptism and then at Ordination, calling you forth to become another Christ. He asked you to arise and go into the abysses, into the man-made hells on earth, and there abide until you are dead, dead to yourselves, dead to the flesh, to pomp and all worldly honours, to all that men hold dear.

Yes, Christ calls you to arise and go into the abysses of man-made hells where few know his awesome, healing, gentle name. There you will find Mary, who abides in all the hells and haunts of men, because as Mother of God, she also is the mother of men.

She will show you her house of love where you must dwell. No matter if that house is far from all that the world cherishes, if it is a bamboo hut, a barge, a cold igloo, a desert tent, or a white, sedate rectory. It remains her house of love, and you must dwell there.

Her priests will begin their life as holocausts for all the priests who do not go, spiritually, to Bethlehem and Nazareth, nor to Gethsemane and the Hill of Skulls. They will be holocausts for those priests who prefer to lead a life of ease with unctuous smiles and holy words spoken with lying lips, who take widows' mites to buy TV sets and golf clubs, and who go on luxurious pilgrimages.

These priests will be holocausts for all the priests who are afraid of men and not of God, for all who revel in pomp and power and are puffed up by it. A holocaust is a sacrifice that must be totally consumed, so that not a shred or speck is left. It has become a complete offering totally consumed.

Yes, they will become holocaust and sacrifice, just like her Son. Passionately, utterly, lovingly, they give themselves as holocausts of *caritas*. For only then will they become men of peace and bring to man-made hells his peace. No one can or will dare to take away his peace from those to whom these priests give themselves.

But holocaust means death, and die they must. A slow and painful death of crucifixion, just like Christ died for them. Men set apart by him, they shall be known as priests of love, mercy and compassion.

V | Loneliness and priesthood

"A priest is a holy man because he walks before the face of the All-Holy."

The loneliness felt by a priest is a gift to me. Here is a priest in the midst of a busy place like Toronto, New York, or Chicago. He may perhaps have a little self pity. He has not thought through whether the loneliness is from himself or from God. Once he comprehends that it is from God, strange things will happen around him. The parish, the people will rally.

We all suffer from loneliness, one way or another. To begin with, we're lonely because we're separated from God, in a manner of speaking. "My heart shall not rest," said Saint Augustine, "until it rests in Thee." The Psalmist says: "I desire to see Your face more than a deer yearns to drink from running streams."

We are meant for God. God thirsts for union with us: a personal love affair. Sooner or later in life we discover that there is in us a garden enclosed, an area of our being where no one can penetrate, a loneliness no one can fill, a longing no one can satisfy.

The experience of that kind of loneliness is really the Holy Spirit calling to us within our own self, saying "In your heart, in your mind's eye, you are running all over the world. Your desires are on the rampage. Now stop that, drop your desires, be quiet, stand still, float down within yourself until you rest in Me, for no one but I can satisfy your longing.

"No one but I can take you out of this kind of loneliness. As you meet and embrace me—your God—you will no longer be lonely. I alone can satisfy your heart and save you from despair or disappointment. You are made for me and there is a part of you which no human being can enter. It is reserved to me. That is where I live, waiting for you to come down within yourself and meet me and I will kiss you with the kiss of my mouth."

Many of us, when experiencing loneliness, seek to compensate by all kinds of false solutions, such as sex, alcohol, drugs, or work. We think that perhaps marriage will fill up that lonely spot. Well, I've been married twice and I can testify that one of the great pains in marriage is that I was never able to probe my husband's heart. There was always a place reserved for God and the entry was closed to me. He had the same feeling when he tried to probe my heart.

When you pray you begin to understand that loneliness is a gift; it is God calling you to himself. As time progresses and the restlessness of youth simmers down, your eyes go inward, inside of yourself, and then you begin to see that someone walked into that garden. You can see footprints in your heart and you follow them and there He is, sitting in your garden, waiting for you.

So when loneliness comes upon you, when you want to go and hide in some corner, when self pity tosses you like a huge wave onto a beach full of stones and you think you are going to be broken up by them, when this happens, close your eyes and repeat: "In my heart there is a garden enclosed." (Sg 4:12) This enclosure is for God, and the waves have brought you into this garden, where the feelings of self pity and anger and all kinds of reactions will disappear. For if you go into that garden, you will hear the incredible sounds that seemingly only one man heard before, the heartbeats of God. (Jn 13:25)

God will enlighten you; he will give you the grace to truly believe in his love for you. God loves us so much. Do we love him back? Are we ready to fall in love with him? Or are we just floating from one place to another like a leaf falling from a tree, wafted by the wind and getting nowhere, but twirling round and round? God is in love with us. Are we in love with him? The only way to assuage loneliness is love.

We are a fragmented people and need recollection and solitude. Through prayer, through listening to the Word of God, we gather our scattered fragments and become whole again. When my loneliness shares the loneliness of Christ, then his peace invades me and we become one.

Now the question is, how do we approach solitude? Do we always need to be with people or are we mature enough to be alone for a little while?

Once we become accustomed to solitude then loneliness can be easily tackled, because solitude is a corridor to God, and Christ was exceedingly lonely. Visualize the second person of the most Holy Trinity living among us. Only an infinite love could make him bear people like Philip, to whom Christ said, "Three years you have walked with me and you still do not understand anything," or words to that effect. Then there was Peter, the impulsive one. Even Our Lady could not understand many things. She pondered them in her heart.

I think that God created loneliness in us so that we might seek beyond our friends, husbands, wives, or communities to enter into his real plan for us. It is by becoming one with the Trinity, which is the uncreated and first community, that we can become one with humanity.

When you become a member of a community, be it a family or a religious or lay community like ours, then solitude leads to a loneliness that is a grace of God, because it is there that the hunger for him takes shape, that the thirst for him becomes unquenchable. Interiorly, we move. We arise and go into the oasis of his heart where he feeds us wine and bread that gives us strength to share the loneliness of others and to lead them to God.

There is a loneliness not given by God but by his opposite. This is the loneliness which begins with the words "I, me, myself, I feel, I am, I want," and so on. When a person spends one hour telling you about themselves, you begin seriously to pray that they should eliminate the pronoun "I" in whatever form it is being used, because a most terrible loneliness can occur to the person who is meeting only himself and adoring himself. I call it the loneliness of mirrors. One is enclosed, as it were, in a kind of mirrored room and no matter where you go, you see yourself and bow to yourself until you go crazy. That is the terrible loneliness of the devil, though it is as easily smashed as mirrors are.

A stone can smash them. Even the eyes of a child can smash them! If the person who is so completely wrapped up in self and his or her own ideas realizes for a split second that this is for the birds, you can hear the cracking of mirrors all over the place. The supersonic barrier opens between man and God.

There is also a strange "in-between" loneliness where I struggle to go where God calls me; it is a sharing in another's aloneness in order to bring him from fragmentation to wholeness, and to direct the face of his loneliness to God.

The weight of God is heavy on all of us. That's why we want to run away from it. God is both so light and so heavy. He's so heavy, because he has allowed us to share with him the weight of his cross. As Saint Paul says: "It makes me happy to be suffering for you now, and in my own body to do what I can to make up all the hardships that still have to be undergone by Christ for the sake of his body, the Church." (Col 1:24)

Who wants to make up the sufferings of Christ? Who wants to walk in the loneliness of the Way of the Cross? of Golgotha? of Gethsemane? And in the loneliness of his life, when the Apostles didn't understand much of what he said? Who wants to?

When faced with loneliness we run here, there and everywhere, trying to escape this monster, not realizing that when we accept it we will learn how much God loves us, and other things as well. Is not his death on the cross proof enough of his love for us?

When will we understand that happiness lies in entering his loneliness? There he will embrace you and console you, providing you accept to be nailed on the other side of his cross. If you do, you will know happiness because the cross is the marriage bed of Christ.

True love enters the portals of loneliness, of total surrender, of forgetting one's self, of thinking only of the other, of remembering that your brother is your life, because your brother is God: "Whatsoever you do to the least of my brethren, you do to me." (Mt 25:41)

When you enter these portals and offer the hospitality not only of your doors but of your heart, and at the same time remain in that loneliness, then you shall know happiness.

The loneliness to which God invites us is a creative loneliness. Priests especially should think about that for they are the loneliest people on earth if you look at it from a human point of view. They have to walk in the darkness of faith and support everybody else and feed everybody else.

The loneliness of God has nothing to do with being single or married, old or young. It is something quite different. No one who loves God is exempt from loneliness because it is one of the deepest ways by which God calls a person to become what he really is: a creative restorer, one who brings beauty and new life to his fellow human being.

What are we all hungering for? No one wants to use the
word. Let us use it: holiness. That is what we hunger for. What
is holiness? Holiness is the forgetfulness of one's self for others.
Deep down in our hearts all of us wish we could be holy.

The way to holiness is loneliness.

God invites us to accept the loneliness of walking alone
with him. He says, "Yes, you need help from other people, but
first get it from me. Attach yourself to me. I will give you
everything you need, for I am the Lord of everything. I will
renew and restore you and you will have new eyes and new
ears. Enter the loneliness of faith and you will become a new
person. You will become new because simultaneously you will
hear my voice and that of those for whom I died. You will see
into their hearts and bring them to me."

The assuaging of this loneliness is a journey inward. And
those of us who try to really love as God asked us to, must be
ready to walk that inward journey with our brothers and sisters.

I want to share your loneliness, dearly beloved Fathers,
because it is one of the reasons why you feel so unsure about
things, especially as your years in the priesthood progress. Yes,
loneliness is yours, but don't you understand that your loneliness is shared with Jesus Christ, with the Trinity. The Apostles
were asleep in Gethsemane when Christ asked them to keep
watch with him. But Christ never sleeps. He is always at your
side and he shares your loneliness.

True, the loneliness will be with you, perhaps always, but
the song of the Trinity will reverberate in your heart and you
will be able to dance to its tune. Joy inexpressible will over-
come the loneliness.

Loneliness shared with Christ, with a deep understanding
as to why you are sharing it, turns to joy. And this is a kind of
joy that stays deep within the priestly heart. It remains there.
It is like a little brook watering the deserts that are so often in
men's hearts, especially priestly hearts.

VI | Why we call you Father

"The heart of a priest is the trysting place of human and divine love."

Long ago, when I was about eleven or twelve, and far away in a convent of the Sisters of Sion in Ramleh near Alexandria, Egypt, a Jesuit priest gave us little ones a talk. He was holy and simple. He touched my young heart deeply. However, I didn't like it when he asked us to pray for priests "when we became a little more grown up." I asked myself, "Why should I wait an eternity—until I reach eighteen or nineteen—to pray for priests?" I spoke privately with the priest and explained my longing to pray for priests at once.

The Jesuit looked intently and earnestly at me and asked if I truly desired to pray for priests. When I responded affirmatively, he placed his hand upon my head, prayed to the Trinity, patted my cheek and said, "Now, I have blessed you so that, young as you are, you can pray for priests. Don't forget to do so, child!"

I have never forgotten that special blessing. Even as a child, I loved priests with my whole heart. In my youthful mind, I firmly believed that Christ left us priests because he didn't want to leave us orphans or to part from us. I didn't understand a great deal about the Mystical Body and the many ways Christ remains in our midst. However, I sensed the very

special role that priests play in Christ's plan and I found it terribly important to pray for them.

I have acted upon that blessing given to me in Egypt so
many decades ago. Except for the period when I with my family was fleeing the communist revolution and I was too sick
and weak to pray (I weighed barely eighty-two pounds), I have,
since the age of twelve, prayed continually for priests.

I have stored up many things in my heart and many feelings, which for so long I was hesitant or afraid to express.
Before Vatican II, there were many sentiments and thoughts
that one simply wouldn't think of expressing. Now, however, at
the age of seventy-seven, I am no longer afraid to face you, my
priests, and to share my heart with you. Though it is difficult
to speak about my personal love for you, I must try.

It is important for us, the laity, to communicate to you,
dear Fathers, both our feelings and our needs. We long to hear
your voices echoing the call of the one Shepherd you represent
so tangibly for us. If we do not hear this voice through you,
how shall we hear it?

Lately, your reassuring voices have either been muted or
simply drowned out by the din of a noisy and confused world.
We need to hear your voices clearly and we need to hear them
now. Our pastures once so green and nourishing for us are
being scorched by the searing heat of materialism, selfishness,
and doubt. Only your voices united with the voice of the Good
Shepherd can lead us to verdant fields once again.

The Prince of Darkness is clouding minds, frightening the
flock, forcing us to huddle together, uncertain of the direction
we must travel in. But in the present twilight we, the laity, are
confident that in the face of danger, dear Fathers, you will
stand by us and lead us.

At Madonna House, we insist on addressing priests as
"Father." Though some prefer to be called simply by their first
name we find it impossible to comply with their wish. We rec-

ognize too clearly the fact that the priest provides for his spiritual family as surely as a father for his natural family. A natural father is a "bread winner." A priest is a "bread giver" in the Eucharist. As children we begin to learn something about God the Father's love for us through experiencing our own father's love for our own family; gradually we learn even more about God's paternal love through your love for all families. Thus we call you "Father."

A father is a man who has begotten children. He has a family he must look after. He must provide the necessities of food, shelter, clothing, education and medical care. He must be present to his family and give them all his love, care and attention. A father is the head of a community of love. Together with his wife, he forms an atmosphere of love conducive not only to healthy human growth but to spiritual growth as well.

Through his example, a father teaches his most effective lessons. It is from his own tender, responsible actions that his children learn the heart and the art of loving. Though loving his own family above all others, a father is also aware of the needs of his neighbours. In fact, according to his state in life and concrete situation, a father is concerned with the needs of the whole world. In all cases, however, a truly loving father is willing to submit his own needs to those of others. This is the ideal we the laity have of fathers.

We call you "Father" because you participate in the one priesthood of Christ. You begot us in the mystery of a tremendous love affair between yourself and God. You are wedded to the Church, his bride. Even should the law of celibacy be rescinded, you will still be wedded to the Church, and it will still have to take precedence over everything in your life.

We call you "Father" and we are your family. We need you desperately. We need you where God has placed you, at the head of our family, just as he has placed human fathers in the midst of their families to nurture and love them.

Whenever an ordinary, human father abandons his family to fulfill his own immediate needs, he creates a truly tragic situation. His entire family, especially his children, are left confused, frightened and lost. The fact that so many human fathers have abandoned their duties accounts for much of the anarchy that has befallen the world. The large number of priests who have abandoned their duties accounts for a great deal of the pain in the Church throughout the world.

Why so many priests have abandoned their spiritual families is difficult to say. Perhaps, under the pressures of changing values, they suddenly placed their own needs before the needs of their family. I would never judge harshly the decision of any priest because I know the pressures and burdens priests bear and the spiritual agonies they encounter. However, remember, dear Fathers, you are not alone. Christ is with you. We, your children, need you.

I would like to suggest, dear Fathers, that you meditate often on the state and plight of the laity you serve. We are young, middle-aged, or elderly. Some of us are married, some single; some well educated and some illiterate; some are rich and some poor. All of us are like the grass, here today and gone tomorrow.

You can identify with the situation of the father of a family. He works hard for his family to fulfill their needs. At times he dreams of greener fields opening up to him. However, if he loves his family he will not follow those dreams if they conflict with the real needs of his loved ones. As monotonous, unsatisfying and painful as this may be, loving fathers respond to the needs of their families by sticking to the task at hand. In spite of the manifold problems that assail their family, things work out. They work out because of love and because of God.

We the laity call you by the awesome name "Father," because we see you attending to our spiritual needs. You were ordained to serve us, to feed us with the Eucharist, to heal us with anointing, to reconcile us to God and one another in penance, to witness our unions of love in marriage, to preach God's word.

We the laity can be healers in many ways. We can be charismatic healers, doctors, psychologists, psychiatrists and social workers. We can even be counsellors to you our priests! However, we cannot heal in the same sacramental sense that you can.

If you carry on your own proper healing ministry, you will inspire us to carry God's saving word into the inner city and the suburbs, to the rich and the poor. We can do all this as long as you preach the Gospel to us and nurture us with the sacraments. We need you present to us wherever you may be assigned. We need to be taught by your patience, your kindness, your understanding and your fortitude, what it is to be a Christian.

Have mercy on us, your ordinary, monotonous, dumpy, unleavened flock! Teach us how to love. Teach us how to pray. Inflame our hearts with the desire to wash the feet of our poor brethren, to feed them love, and to preach the Gospel with our lives. Send us forth everywhere: into the world of poverty, hunger, and misery, so that we may change it because we heard your voice sending us there—the Shepherd's voice.

Come with us if God appoints you to do so. Lead us wherever he tells you. But do not desert us in order to fulfill personal ambition or your own immediate needs. In doing God's will you fulfill your deepest needs and longings.

The endless pursuit of new life styles or academic degrees and recognition is not the way to priestly happiness. If you follow the voice of the Shepherd and pursue his values you will find peace. True, there will be turmoil in your life, just as there was turmoil in the life of every prophet and in the life of the Divine Master himself. Nevertheless, there will be that unshakable tranquility that comes from knowing that you are doing God's will and not your own.

The prophets of old were seized with the desire to preach God's word, to teach his people. They emptied themselves for the sake of the people. They spent themselves in God's service meeting the needs of others. They gave up secular pursuits to dedicate themselves to the ministry of the word. Be careful, dear Fathers, not to abandon your priestly duties for worldly interests. Never be so taken up with the material aspects of your life (taking care of Church property, raising funds, and so on) that you neglect your spiritual duties. Never be so enamored with lay life styles as to abandon your priesthood altogether.

I would like to tell you clearly, dear Fathers, that any overpowering urge to fulfill your own needs at the expense of the needs of your flock, your spiritual family, does not come from God. The sense of urgency and immediacy to change everything at once to suit your own tastes or inclinations does not spring from the eternally patient, all-loving God.

You may want to do noble deeds and accomplish much. You might like to become a psychologist or a foreign missionary. Yet the most important question is not what you want, but what God wants for you. If you want to become a psychologist or a foreign missionary to fulfill your own needs, you will not be satisfied either as a priest or as a person.

The impatience to fulfill yourself and your desires can only spring from our fallen nature or the Prince of False Promises. Perhaps, in a scientific age it seems foolish to consider the Prince of Darkness. But as I nightly pray and agonize over the problems that beset you, the priests I love so dearly, I hear, figuratively speaking, the barely audible, slithering movements of a serpent. The sound of that slithering serpent will be with us until the end of time. As long as we desire to do our own will rather than God's, the sound will haunt us. It is frightening to hear that sound but even more frightening to see some of God's priests apparently following that sound with its promises that are so shallow.

Only the path of prayer can help us in this situation or any like it. When you bow your head in prayer and ask the Lord for guidance, dear Father, realize that you are not praying alone but that countless people who rely on you are praying with and for you.

Have you pondered the Book of Numbers? I was reading it recently. In it there is the question of the census of the tribes, and I came to the statute for the Levites: "The Levites are to pitch their tents around the tabernacle of the Testimony. In this way the wrath will be kept from falling on the whole community of the sons of Israel. The Levites are to be in charge of the tabernacle of the Testimony."

A little further down I read, "Yahweh spoke to Moses and said: 'I myself have chosen the Levites from among the sons of Israel, in place of the firstborn, those who open the mother's womb among the sons of Israel; these Levites therefore belong to me.'"

Again I read: "Take the Levites in the place of all the first-born of Israel's sons, and the cattle of the Levites in place of their cattle; the Levites shall be my own, Yahweh's own." This made me think of priests. This statute of the Levites simply expresses an ideal, it seems to me, that flowered into the Christian priesthood of today.

It is a confirmation for one who constantly thinks of the priesthood with much love and tenderness and compassion. Obviously, the priest of today must "pitch his tent next to the tabernacle of Testimony." This means, according to my understanding, that he must keep his heart close to the Word of God, to the Gospel of Jesus Christ.

Have you meditated on that, my beloved Fathers? The priest of today should remember that word, for if he doesn't, the wrath of God is going to descend on all his people. It tears my soul apart, and I feel swords within me, as I think that more and more priests have left their tents, the sides flapping loudly to a wind that didn't come from heaven. The priests of today, even as the Levites of old, take the place of the first-born, in this case, Jesus Christ!

Therefore I brought with me wherever I went, the custom of standing up for priests when they enter a room. For in truth each one is Jesus Christ. Yahweh said so himself when he spoke of the Levites and their role.

Somehow this meditation that took place one night made my prayers for priests more fervent than before. I was beseiged with an urgency to implore the Lord to stop the leakage of priests. Everything became so tremendously clear regarding the role of the priests, above all the fact that they were God's special property and hence intensely blessed by him. In his eyes they were his first-born and they were to dwell near him in their tents. For what is the altar of Testimony but himself? As the glories of the priesthood invaded my heart I cried out, "Lord, let them see who they are. Don't let them wander away into the dark wind that doesn't come from heaven."

All the time I also knew that God already is sending his grace, his charisms, his love, his very self into priests everywhere, but that he would never interfere with their free will. This is fantastic: the all-powerful God has put a restriction upon himself and limited his power so that we human beings may truly be free. Incredible, isn't it?

God has chosen you to live close, very close, to the altar of Testimony, in order to understand that you belong to God, that you are his property; to know in great depth that you are his first-born. This faith knowledge is given to you so that you might preach it, give it, offer it, in the chalice of the tenderness of your love and compassion to other priests.

Yes, dear Fathers, every word of this very botched-up chapter was torn out of my heart while I prayed at night for all priests. No one writes too well with fragments of her heart.

VII

You bring us joy

"A priest is a lover of God, a priest is a lover of men."

Dear Fathers, do you realize that you are a joy to the world? At Christmas we sing *Joy to the World* and other songs and carols expressing our gladness in the coming of Christ, and we feel an absolute burst of joy when he comes. Did it ever occur to you that the same sentiments and feelings come to our hearts when you visit our homes?

In the old days, of course, people prepared for your coming by polishing and cleaning everything. That may have lessened a bit, but today, like yesterday, the joy is still there. To have a priest come and visit us—well, that's quite something! For those of us who have faith and who understand a little, it is the coming of Christ. We hear the knock or the doorbell, and someone says, "Father is coming," and we rush to the door. This may seem a little old fashioned to you, especially to young priests. But even if you don't see these things happening to you, don't kid yourself. They do happen in the hearts of the young and the old.

You are a bringer of joy. When you come to visit the sick there is some kind of uplift and hope springs forth. Not necessarily that the sick will not die, no. But some strange, unaccountable joy takes hold of people. I have seen it over and over again. Working in a hospital, I have seen the faces of patients light up. Into their eyes came an expectancy not seen before, not even when their husbands or wives, fathers, mothers, brothers or sisters came. It was an expectancy that seemed to exclaim, "Oh, Father is here. I can put my soul into his hands and I can lay my head (figuratively speaking) on his shoulder."

You see, the joy that you bring is manifold, and if you only had time to spend with us you would realize how beautiful it is. If only you had time to see in our faces the joy that your coming creates, you would find yourself praising the Lord with all your soul.

Even when you might not bring good news—natural good news—it doesn't seem to matter. You bring supernatural joys. Suppose (and I have seen it happen) a priest comes to tell a daughter that her mother has died, a wife that her husband has died; or a mother that an accident has happened and her children were killed. When you are the person who brings the sad news, somewhere deep in those broken hearts arises the Good News of Christ. Did you ever think about that?

I had a patient who was very sick. She was always glad when a priest came for a few minutes to say hello to her, to hold her hand, to cheer her up. But one day this priest met me at the door of the ward and said, "I'm afraid to walk up to the door of Mrs. So–and–so because I have to give her the news that her husband died. He fell from the fifteenth floor." He was a construction worker. I said, "Father, you must not be afraid because you bring to her the will of God and it will be her sanctification and yours."

He looked at me a little strangely but went and told her, and I stayed nearby. She screamed and fainted. We revived her. Then she cried. At the end she said, "Well, perhaps Peter is better off, for he is now with God. The Lord said so. He had a good life, Peter. He loved the Lord so he is alright now. It is myself that I should weep for, not him." The priest was simultaneously the bearer of natural bad news and supernatural Good News. That is one of your joys.

But you have so many joys, dear Fathers. You know, because you have looked into the eyes of the children to whom you teach catechism. Isn't it beautiful to look at the limpid eyes of very young children who have not yet been touched by the evil one? You must have a voice singing inside of you when you look at those children, for reflected in their black eyes, blue eyes, gray eyes, green eyes, is Jesus Christ. What immense joy is yours! And what joy you give them! Did you ever notice, (unless some strict adult is present) how they run up to you and say, "Father! Father! Father!" Just those voices, and the name they call you, must lift your soul up high and allow it to sing as David sang before the altar.

At times you probably envy, momentarily, the people whose marriages you witness. The thought of the natural bliss which they will share and which you have foregone can be painful. Yet, could it possibly be that a strange, quiet and holy joy enters your heart as you bless the wedded pair? Suddenly you realize the very essence of celibacy. Suddenly, as if God opened some kind of door in his own heart, you understand why you are a celibate: because your celibacy lights a candle before God on his altar, before his sanctuary.

For a strange moment you see yourself—a candle lit by God. Yes, God has sent the fire, and why did he send the fire but that it should embrace the whole earth. You are the beginning of that fire. A tiny, little light on a candle. You can look at yourself when the bridal couple has departed. You are a celibate. You are virginal. Even if you are a widower, you are virginal at this moment. You are like the virginal wax of the bees, burning yourself up for Christ's sake. Because you are who you are, our heads bow. This kind of chastity for the sake of Christ is holy.

You are the candle of atonement. You are the fire that Christ uses to light in a young soul the heroism which cries, "Lord, I throw my life at your feet and sing and sing that I bring you such a small thing!" This chastity of yours is a fantastic help for the rest of us.

But have you noticed how the joy of your presence—our joy in being around you—has diminished lately? Perhaps it is partly because some have embraced the married state and have left the altar. I wonder if their memory of what they were has not lain heavily on them.

Something really struck me several years ago. I read in a Russian paper that the priests to be ordained petitioned their Patriarch for celibacy. But the Patriarch refused them because their parishioners would not understand unmarried priests. There were some four hundred of them, so it said in the paper. At the same time I read that many hundreds of priests petitioned the pope to give them the right to marry.

There is nothing wrong with being married, providing you go through the proper channels. But do you know something, dear Fathers? The joy that you have now will be different if and when you are allowed to be married. I cannot quite explain this.

Even today somehow, there is an abundant joy, a singing joy, a dancing joy, in the hearts of your people when they know that you have kept the vow of celibacy, come hell or high water. Because they know it is for them that you have kept it, and the joy spreads amongst your people because it comes from you.

We need the joy. In the darkness of our age, in the jungle in which we live, we need the candle of your joy, the candle that stands in the candlestick of faith, love, poverty, chastity and all that a priest is or should be.

Yes, dear Fathers, you do not realize how much joy your very presence brings. How much hope it brings, too! As usual, after my many years of contacts with people, I have another story to tell!

I had a spiritual director, Father Keating, a Jesuit. He was then Provincial of the Jesuits in Toronto and lived not far from us, maybe four or five blocks away, on Portland Street, where we had our Friendship House—right by the railroad yards. The Jesuits bought the place from the Loretto Sisters who moved uptown. So I went to the place quite often, both for spiritual direction and just to chat a little.

One day I heard that Father was kind of run down and that the doctor ordered him to take a walk everyday, for at least an hour, and more if possible. The doctor was adamant that he should walk, even in all kinds of weather—except for downpours or blizzards. The doctor told him how far he should walk.

Well, I went to commiserate with Father and to cheer him up, but I also had another idea. I said to him, "Father Keating, since you have to walk three miles a day, why not walk in the slums, right where you are?" In those days the place was not so polluted. The Toronto air was fresh. So he might as well walk where he lived.

He said, "Why should I walk around this place? I should go to the park or some place away from here." But I replied, "You know, because I have told you many times, both in confession and out, how I worry about Cameron Street. It is filled with Communists. Why not walk on Cameron Street? They may throw stones at you but I am sure they would be very little stones. They won't harm you. And you will bring hope to people in the neighbourhood, because a priest brings hope. Just your walking down these streets, where ninety-four percent of the people belong to the Communist party, will somehow or other bring hope."

He looked at me. Being my spiritual director, he knew me very well. He said, "Catherine, you certainly have the Russian ability of building castles in Spain." "Oh," said I, "I have more!

I am already making like we are in the parousia. Why not dream about what is inevitably going to happen?"

Father teasingly asked me if I was absolutely sure that I would enter the parousia, that is to say, paradise. Perhaps I might enter some other place! I said, "Now, now, Father. You are my spiritual director. Would you consign me to hell? Or to purgatory?" "Well," he replied, "a spiritual director never discusses such things with a spiritual directee." Thus we sidetracked the purgatory business neatly as only Jesuits can!

Anyhow, he said, "Okay, I'll walk, but I don't quite believe that I am a sign of hope." I said, "The Lord will show you. You forget who you are. Jesuits, Franciscans, secular priests or Carmelites, you forget who you are or perhaps you don't even realize who you are. This is going to show you that you are a sign of hope." I knelt for his blessing and disappeared.

Thereafter, everyday between four and six o'clock, I saw Father walking the slum streets, especially Cameron Street, and, as I predicted, little stones, not big ones, hit his coat but never his face. A few words about being a hypocrite and that sort of thing were hurled out of the windows at him, but he was six-foot-one and very strong looking, besides being handsome. He was about fifty or so. He had presence.

The seasons rolled on. Fall came and went, and then the snowflakes fell. One day a woman ran out from a little house, looked around to see if anybody was watching, then whispered to Father, "Pray for my son. He is very sick." And she scuttled back again.

When Father dropped in at Friendship House he said, "Maybe you are right. Maybe I am a sign of hope." Well, thereafter the woman came out to him again and again. One day he very quietly put a blessed medal in her hand, a medal of Our Lady of La Salette. Then she ran back again.

About a week later she returned, standing straight, not running, not afraid of anybody. She took Father's hand and kissed it according to the beautiful Slavic custom, and said, "My son is well, thanks to your prayers."

I am almost afraid to ask this, but I must: Do you have that kind of faith? Have you looked at yourself and understood who you really are? Oh, you might be Tom, Dick or Harry. You might be fat, thin, old or young. You can look in a mirror until the mirror falls down, but you will not see in a mirror who you really are. It's when your eyes are turned to the heart of Christ, who is your real mirror, that you will see that you are another Christ, with all his powers, amongst them the power of giving hope, joy, faith and love.

Yes, believe it or not, when you are around you are a sign of hope. You may neither feel that you are nor know that you are, but you are. Be careful not to let this gift slip through your fingers, for in the soul of a human being hope is a fragile thing, and the laity has been led to so many dead ends with slogans like, "God is here. God is there. Come here. Go there," when they have been lies. People will approach you sometimes as if you also were a liar and a hypocrite. At times anger will spill upon you because someone has betrayed the most precious thing: God in a human soul.

So remember: you are a sign of hope. You are a sign of joy. You live on the street of broken dreams but you lead people to God who alone can repair them. With his power you can, too. God and you are good repairmen. Perhaps in our century you could call it a recycling of hearts. Be that as it may, you are a sign of hope.

VIII |  *Alter Christus* — another Christ

"A priest is the symbol of the Word made flesh."

A talk to priests.

Most of you I know personally, or have met before, and as men you are my friends; yet when I see you together like this I have a tremendous sense of Christ's priesthood. Because there is only one priesthood: his. In this room there is a presence of Christ with an overwhelming power, because all of you are in that priesthood.

I wonder if you give this much thought: that the tremendous powers you have are not for yourself. He gave them to you for us, for all people, for other priests, but especially for us, your flock. You walk in such blinding light that it is almost impossible, in faith, to look at it. God loves you with an everlasting love and he has chosen you—ordinary men—to bring us God and show us his love.

Jesus desired with passionate desire to remain with his flock. So he multiplies himself in other men through his priesthood, because he could not leave us; and the great miracle of his staying with us is the Eucharist—which we could not have without you, his priests. Only a lover who is God could give us a gift like this. He is the fantastic Lover who spills his love over the whole of history.

I look at you, and in faith I see a beautiful sight. I see Christ taking me in his arms and consoling me while I weep at his feet in the confessional. I see Christ feeding me with his Body. It is his lips which pronounce the words of Consecration while his hands hold the Host. I can touch his hands in yours; I kiss his hands when I kiss yours. And when I am sick, and darkness closes in on me, and fear enters my heart, who comes? Christ! *You* come, but it is really Christ who comes to me.

What we wish from you so passionately, what we hunger for with such a tremendous hunger, is that you give us God, not yourself! We have thousands of people who can counsel us. We have thousands who can give us psychiatric help. We can have many, many friends if we wish. But our hunger for God transcends all other hungers. Give us God, because he has called you to be himself, to act like he did, to do what he did. Sit on the grass with us, teach us the Beatitudes, go with us into our homes—poor, rich or whatever they may be. Do not try to bring us to yourself; bring us to God through yourself.

There are many new theologies. The laity are taking courses in theology, and there is much discussion about it all. But do you know how love is taught? What theology really is? They tell me that *theos* means God, and that theology is the science of our God. I don't like that word "science," because there is no science about God. God is too infinite to be approached by any kind of scientific method.

The only way to approach God is by love. There is no other way, because he isn't a subject of the intellect. You can use your intellect, of course; you have to use it. But don't stop there, because you will never know God that way.

And so it seems to me that a priest is, above all, a lover, but a very strange lover. How we need love that is taught to us by example, not by words! Words are a babble of tongues around our ears today. Every priest seems to have another idea about what Christianity is; but his words don't echo Christ's words. They don't do for our souls what they should be doing.

A priest is truly another Christ. What does it mean to be another Christ? It means to do as he did. I don't think he had any techniques. But he was able to talk to slaves, to Jews, to Gentiles, to big-shots and little-shots, to all people, in the language they needed to hear. Something about Christ in the priest is strength-giving in my own journey to Christ, when the priest tries to be Christ as much as he can at the moment, with a cry to heaven for grace to be more so every day. Love speaks more clearly than techniques.

We need priestly concern about ourselves. We, the laity, are small, even in this time of the lay apostolate. We are like children in a desert, today especially. Too many voices attack us, too many ideas are pushed into us. We are lost somewhere and we need the clear, simple voice of Christ to say: "Only one thing matters. What would it profit to gain the whole world if you lose your soul?" Tell us about the one thing necessary, but especially show it to us.

We are bewildered, many of us; many of us are filled with hostility to authority and all it entails. You often are, too. You may be hostile to your bishops or to priests in authority. Many lay people today are hostile to all priests and to the Church. Many young people are hostile because of various painful influences in their lives. They are just tired of authority which has often been wielded in wrong ways. Maybe you feel that way about the pastor, the bishop, or someone else.

However, all of us have to go to the essence of things. What is that essence? Well, Christ was obedient to the will of the Father. Do we, or do we not believe that we have to live by faith and do the same? To live by faith is to live in a mystery, often the strange mystery of darkness where the terrors of the night get hold of you until you can't stand it any more; where the bitter waters of rivers seem to engulf you; when the fire, far from merely touching you, sears you.

These are times of crisis, times of chaos, times of Towers of Babel that are invisible but higher than the one built in the Old Testament. We have to have a point of beginning again. We laity have to hold onto something. We are the flock. You are covered with the fullness of Christ's priesthood.

Do you really believe with an unshakable faith that you are another Christ in the theological sense of the word? Or is that a secondary idea?

Are you aware that this house is blessed by your presence? Are you aware that you are blessing these hills and everybody around you? Are you? Are you aware of what it means when you bless us after dinner? Do you see with the eyes of faith the light that goes through us when you do? Can you hear Christ's voice with an Aramaic accent blessing and teaching us through you with an English accent? Are you aware of this? We are. But because you don't always act as if you were aware, the laity sometimes reject you, especially the youth.

The question is: Is faith real to us today? Having talked to many, many people this year, I begin to think that we just don't live by faith. We live by everything but faith. So we miss the tenderness of God. I speak for all the laity when I say that what we want is the tenderness of God. Young, old or middle aged, we are lonely. The loneliness of this generation is a tragedy, and you are a bridge that allows each island to have transportation to another.

Talk to us about the love of God. Talk to us about *your* love of God. Tell us how difficult it is; we will understand. We will come and love with you. Into you he pours his love, fills you with it, so that you may feed us—first with himself and then with his love, into which your love for us blends. We need you so. You are the most important people in the Church today. If you fail, as you obviously will because you are human, we are behind you to pray for you, to uphold you. But don't leave us orphans; because the night is dark and the terrors are frightening for us, especially for the young.

There is something here so deep, so profound. I feel as if I am fumbling like a three year old child playing with toy bricks. I want to tell you something and I cannot because there are no words to tell you the things that have to be told. This is the crisis of the Church. The Church is you and I, the spouses of Christ. Are we going to tear her apart, or are we going to put her together? Which is it going to be? It depends upon you. In your humble, sinful hands the Lord really put the fate of the world today—the Catholic Christian world.

We need you. Show us the way, but walk it with us; don't just tell us how to walk it. Walk it, and we will follow you. Don't just teach us verbally to do this or that. Do it! Show us! The most effective lesson is seeing the message lived.

I stumble in trying to express myself, because the agony, the anxiety, the anguish of the Church and of humanity is in my heart. I can smell the dust in India. I am with the woman who gives birth on that dusty road. I am that farmer who doesn't know where his next meal is coming from. I am that man dying of cancer. I am the million young people who don't know where to go because nobody shows them the way.

It is essential for the priest to be a friend to youth and to everybody, but there is a dignity about it. The heart of a priest is like a well-tuned violin, or some kind of lyre, that reverberates and continually gives us the echo of God's voice because he is listening to it with his whole being—his body, psyche, and mind. He is in Christ because he wants to give Christ. He is an ordinary, weak mortal in an immense *mysterium*, clad with the power of God beyond his own imagining.

Only in truth, whose other name is humility, can a priest see the immense powers that he has been given, that are his because he is Christ. And, if he uses that power with the simplicity of a child and the love of a lover, a friend and a brother of God, then miracles of moving mountains will be child's play to him, for he lives in the tremendous light of a dark faith.

The agony of people today is indescribable, and there will be times when priests will want to run away. I was taught by my parents from childhood to open my heart to everybody, but I never knew then what an agony it can be to do so. I can understand priests wanting to run away, because in order to make room for the humanity in each person (and each represents Christ to us), we must allow Christ himself to come into us. And since he comes in his entirety, it seems as though he tears us apart. Only his love can enable us to sustain his presence.

So you must make room for Christ and for all of humanity. And one can't seek a return for love. Christ wasn't exactly loved. His apostles were a bunch of pretty rough men who didn't understand much. It must have been very difficult for Christ to be patient with them. After three years Philip still didn't get the picture. And after his resurrection, Christ chided them because they were still hard-headed and stiff-necked and didn't understand.

How many friends did Christ have? A handful; and on the cross he was abandoned by most of them. That will also be the picture of the man, the woman, the Christian who lets humanity into his or her heart. No, we must not expect gratitude or a return, but we must love with the passionate love of God, for Christ said: "By this you shall be known as my disciples, that you love as I have loved you."

How can we human beings love with the heart of God? Only by a total surrender. And who manifests the supreme, total surrender amongst us? The one chosen by Christ to hang on the other side of his cross—his priest.

This doesn't exclude working for justice, fighting the good fight, facing the issues in the Church, doing what you must in this post-Conciliar age of open windows, fresh air and beauty.

But all must be done in charity. Love is like a tremendous light in both the Old and the New Testament. Christ has come and told us to love him, both directly and through others. He also said: "Learn of Me for I am meek and humble of heart." And, "What does it profit a man to gain the whole world and suffer the loss of his soul?"

A priest is a man to whom I can go and in whose lap I can place all my burdens. He is the Simon to my passion, to the passion of the world, while he is also the Christ in that passion. He takes upon himself the crucifixion and at the same time he carries the cross for his flock.

He is available to the point of no return in this age when everybody is for himself. He is truly like a pilgrim, not attached to anything. Today in our age of free sex, materialism, comfort, status, we need pilgrims—and I don't mean people without houses. I mean persons who are detached from all possessions, detached from honours, from any return of love, because they are lovers a la Christ. They will love even unto death in spite of everything.

The priest is also a straw in troubled waters. He is our pin-point of light in a darkness that seemingly has no beginning and no end. He is a man. We are not shocked by anything he does, nor by his sins. We are shocked only when he doesn't love and doesn't believe. If he doesn't show us faith and the love of Christ, then we are shocked, because he sells us down the river. His sins don't bother us. His weaknesses don't bother us. We need faith, for everything is dark, and the light of faith must be given to us.

But we must pray with you and for you, and you must pray for us, and we will all grow in faith together. God wants us to grow speedily in the faith given to us at baptism; he wants us to really beg for that faith so that he might have the joy of making us grow swiftly in it. We have to pray for faith until darkness becomes light and fear leaves us. We want to be taught that perfect love that casts out fear. We are not saying that you priests have it. We are saying let's ask God for it together.

Above all, we want to see in you another Christ, because his face is becoming dimmer to us. There is so much noise and so many pictures flashing all over. Have I a great idea of a priest? Oh no, I have the idea of my faith! With an unshakable faith I believe in who you are, what you are, and in your powers. Nobody can move me from that, Deo gratias! Not even yourselves who may not believe in yourselves. I know who you are, and I beg you to look at yourself in the mirror of Christ's eyes. Then you will see who you are. But in order to do so you will have to be very close to him.

So when you love God you obviously look at him with the eyes of faith, and he reveals himself as ever more beautiful, ever more understandable, ever more tender, ever more strong. Now he begins to draw you. Now you enter into him. Now you begin to know who you are in a way that no book can tell you. You know who you are and who he is, and what love is. Now you don't need to read any books. Now you don't need to have men or women friendships. Now you are free with the freedom of the children of God. But the only place that you are going to find that is at his feet. There is no other place.

Don't try to give us what others can give us. Give us what nobody else can give us—give us God. For this you have been ordained, and for nothing else. When you give us God you give us love, a love that this world doesn't know because it is God's love. You will know joy the likes of which men have never dreamed.

IX Protect the Church

"The heart of a priest is pierced, like Christ's, with the lance of love."

One November night I spent many sleepless hours. I was taken up with a deep inner vision that gripped me without ceasing. There is no use beating around the bush: I was in the throes of a sadness beyond description, a fear beyond telling, a numbness. And yet a clarity of mind blended strangely with this.

It came to me that the Catholic Church was in grave danger. With our cold hearts, we the people of God were like a snowball rolling down an immense mountain, becoming gigantic as it rolled. This huge snowball crashed at the foot of the mountain, and the Church lay in ruins underneath the freezing snow which seemed to symbolize the cold hearts of so-called Christians.

As the night passed, within me grew the conviction that the Church is at a crossroads. And that the Church, who is of course us—bishops, priests and lay people—is also the Bride of Christ, the Mystical Body of Christ, of which he is the head. Yes, the Church is so much more than the people of God.

It seemed to me that we are beginning to treat the Church as if it were only human. We are throwing the Church back and forth as if it were a basketball. At the same time, it seemed to me in the dark of that night, that many of us were tearing apart the humanness of the people of God. Conversations were constantly about the errors of the pope, of priests, bishops, nuns, and ourselves too. And our eyes were constantly roaming to find a substitute for what we had deserted.

I realized in that strange night of mine that if we tear that Body, in some inexplicable way the Head will die. It came to me that the Head will die again, that we will re-crucify Christ again in ourselves. The word re-crucify hit me so hard that I seemed to lose all senses, but they returned, and with them fear—fear for us who were treating the Church, his Spouse, in such a manner. Fear shook me like a fever, for I suddenly heard and understood the anger of the Father at the re-crucifixion of his Son, at this total forgetfulness of Catholics of the awesome mystery of the Church which is his Son, who is at once the Head and Bridegroom.

Our faith teaches us that our God is also "a jealous God." He is concerned about our ultimate as well as our present happiness, tranquility and peace, for God loves us, his creatures, simply because God is God.

It came to me, therefore, that God's anger was just, because we were tearing ourselves apart, destroying our peace. God was angry about our blind, absurd, willful, evil ways of treating the immense graces that he sends through the Holy Spirit. God's anger is always his mercy!

God was giving us signs. He was writing some mysterious words on the wall as he did once upon a time in the Old Testament. They were awesome words of warning, of calamity besetting the world, like floods. But more than scientifically explainable words, he was writing on those walls about the terrible, unholy wars that rage, one against the other, in men's souls. For it is in the souls of men that wars begin.

The fragmentation and division of the people of God, their hostility toward one another, their rejection of the gospel—these were before me in stark and fearsome clarity during the night.

Of course, I fully understood that the Church will continue to exist and that all hell will not prevail against it. Nevertheless, I shuddered and almost wept at the responsibility of my brothers and sisters in Christ, and my own as well. For the ones who tear the Church apart are our elite—people endowed by God with graces and talents beyond average.

I trembled, I repeat, at their misuse of their talents and the shirking of true responsibility, especially by priests. In this horrible night of mine these words came to me: "Woe to those who scandalize the little ones of Christ." The priests, instead of leading the little ones to God, instead of making the way easy for them to find him, were either leading them away from him or confusing them by leading them to themselves.

True, there was a Goliath to be killed, but it could only be killed by another David, a simple shepherd boy using as weapons a sling-shot of love and the pebbles of simplicity, humility and childlikeness.

I saw the priests clad in the garments of service, which are the priestly robes of Christ. Next to their sling-shot of love, and the pebbles of humility and simplicity, they all had a towel and a pitcher of water and a basin to wash the feet of all men who came to them. Those who went down from the mountain of the Lord to the valleys of the world carried nothing with them except the sling-shot of charity and the pebbles of childlikeness and humility. They were girded with a towel, knowing that they would find a pitcher and a basin and the clear waters of love flowing from their heart wherever they went to witness to Christ.

Yes, such was the strange November night I spent in some unknown year, half-awake, half-asleep. I still feel as if something tragic is happening. I can almost hear the devil laugh.

Once a woman was caught in adultery. She was brought to Jesus and was about to be stoned. Jesus turned to her accusers and challenged them with the words, "If one of you is without sin, go ahead and stone her." Her accusers had enough self understanding and self knowledge to walk away. They were aware of their own sinfulness and imperfection.

Now it is not surprising that the Church, which is made up of human beings, is imperfect in many ways. However, the Church is faithful in her teaching. Objectively, the woman caught in adultery was spared by her sinful accusers and pardoned by the sinless Christ. In her spotless heart of doctrine and faith the Church of Christ has throughout the centuries remained innocent. We, who are far from innocent as individuals, should therefore be careful not to stone the Church which gives us life.

The pope cherishes the Church as a whole and each of us as individuals. At night he prays for discernment and during the day for wisdom. Dear Fathers, if you truly love the Church, as I know you do, you will unite your prayers with his and neither you nor he will ever be alone in your ministering to God's people. Love is spiritual. It is not thwarted by distances. Be united in spirit with the shepherds.

Thank God that lately it has been a little more quiet. Perhaps the Church is gathering her rags and sewing them up, because we have torn her garments and left the rags all over the place. She might be sewing the rags together. Well, it's good to belong to a ragged Church, but it's not good to make the Church ragged as some theologians do!

Enter into the Holy of Holies, my dearly beloved Fathers. Do! Here is the door. Here is the handle, beautifully wrought. Open it. You have spent many years studying all that there is to be studied about God. But do you know the God who is beyond all study, beyond all approaches of the human mind? Have you opened that door? Have you come through it? Once you have, your words, your deeds and your writing mellow and mature.

I beg you, you who have opened the door and entered into the Holy of Holies, be reverent. The only way that we know God is on our knees, our mind completely empty and put into our heart, our mouth closed. When we are like that, a mystery can slowly, slowly unfold. This requires silence, solitude and so many other things that Our Lady can teach us.

Theology used to be the mistress of all sciences, and still is to those who understand. But what has happened? What has happened to this pure fountain given by God to man? I'll tell you what happened. Throughout history and in our own time as well, man has put his peanut brain into that pure fountain and polluted it!

Dear Fathers, give us the truth. Don't give us theology seasoned with *your* salt. It has no flavour. Give us God's theology. Since theology is the study about God then for God's sake pray that God gives you himself, and then you can give him to us. We are hungry for God as few have been hungry over the centuries.

The Church is an incredible, incomprehensible, untouchable, unassailable mystery that brings men by baptism into the very Body of Christ. Having died with Christ and having risen with him, the Christian becomes one with the Trinity. Who can express *that* mystery? Who can do something about it by himself or by herself? It comes from God.

The Church is the Bride of Christ, spotless, without wrinkle. The Church is you and I, full of sin and sorrow, evil and good. But when her founder, Jesus Christ, became human, the Church was divinized by him.

"By this shall men know that you are my disciples. Love one another as I have loved you." A fantastic mystery is presented to us: to love as God loves. "Zeal for my Father's house burns in me like a flame." This is what God is offering us.

But now I speak of the human Church, ourselves and the hierarchy. I read some years ago how a woman was stabbed in the streets of Brooklyn. A lot of people were watching from their windows. I am afraid that there are an awful lot of people who are watching the Church and hoping that it will be killed some place, in some corner, perhaps forever, and that no one will go to its rescue, as no went to that woman who was killed in the sight of many.

This cannot be! This is the moment in our lives, in our Christian lives, in which we must arise and be inflamed with "zeal for our Father's house." We have the Advocate in us, the Wind that fans this flame that the Scriptures talk about. It is indeed time. I feel like imploring, like weeping, like crying out, like doing a thousand things that people do when they feel close to despair, except that I can't come close to despair because I live in hope.

But I am human and so I cry out, and I think that other lay people cry out with me. Do you hear us? It's not enough to speak softly anymore. We have to cry out. So, filled with hope, yet not far from despair, I howl.

Howl, my soul, howl!
Cry to the Lord for his Church!

Howl, my soul, howl!
For you are plunged in the agony
of his Bride!

Look! See how she is torn asunder!
How her members mock,
ridicule her,
laughing their hellish laughter
as they trample her
into the mire of their twisted souls!

Howl, my soul, howl
before the Lord
as tortured men howled on medieval racks!
For those who are thy people
are trying to make a harlot
of thy Bride!

Howl, howl, howl, my soul!
Cry out the agony which is hers
for you are she!

Howl, my soul, howl,
like men lost in the desert
howl before dying of thirst.
Howl, howl my soul, howl!

Howl!
The time for "crying out of the depths"
is past.
The time for howling is now!

For men are deaf to all words,
deaf to the crying and weeping
of other men.
Yet perhaps the howling
of a soul in agony for your Church
will reach them.
For, as yet, here in this country of the empty rich,
howling has not yet been heard!

So howl in a whisper
like a person dying of hunger.
Howl in a whisper
that in its loudness

enters the mystery of Christ's passion,
circling a world which says
he is dead!

Howl, my soul, howl.
Like a woman howls
at the bedside of her lover or child
when she is past speech or tears!

Howl, my soul, howl,
so that the Lord
may hear the song of pain, of agony
beyond human agony.
For it is he who will be howling in me.

Howl, my soul, howl!
For the Church is in pain.
Look, she lies in the dust of a thousand roads.
No one stops; the Good Samaritan is not yet seen
at the bend of these roads.

Howl, my soul, howl!
Ask Yahweh
to give you the strength
to lift the Church
into the arms of his Son.

Howl, howl my soul, howl!

If you understood the depth of the need that we have for
you, beloved Fathers, which is almost impossible to explain,
you would begin to understand our cry for understanding. You
would understand my poem.

We are in a diaspora and yet we don't have to be. We are joined together by the Holy Spirit because we are baptized; because we have partaken and are constantly partaking of the Eucharistic Banquet; and because the kiss of Christ, in the Sacrament of Confession, kisses us clean again and again, a thousand times over.

So how is it that we are not gathering our forces to counteract those who continue to infiltrate the Church; forces which arise even from within the Church to manipulate her. There is one way to counteract them, and only one way: the way of holiness. For this we were born—to be holy. We are given, by the Church, every advantage in following the path of the Holy One who calls himself "the Way."

The priest is a shepherd. He has a flock given him by God. For this he was ordained. God asks from his priests one thing: that he cleanse his own soul, that he walk the path of the Holy One. Now he falls down, now he bruises himself, but the path was made by God, and so God is around and will help the priest to stand up and to continue walking.

It is almost impossible to express the anguish, the agony, the love that many of us, the laity, feel for the Church. We know that the Church is us. But since many of us have been in the business world, have been married, have been in all kinds of positions of authority and subjection, we realize that we need leaders. We need you, such as you are, as far as your humanity is concerned. I repeat again that it doesn't matter if you are fat or thin. It doesn't matter if you have a beard or not. Nothing matters except that you know who you are, and that you show us that you know who you are.

Come, help us to protect the Church, which is ourselves and you and the hierarchy.

How can you teach me to love my enemy if you publicly attack your bishop or your superior whom you consider to be your enemy? No one amongst us wants to enter into the difficulties that you may have with your superiors, but all of us who love the Church weep when you break Christ's law of love. We don't know where to turn any more. The shepherd is not there, and the sheep are huddling together in the rain, the snow and the cold.

My heart tells me, and it is almost an obsession, that we must get together to protect the Church. There doesn't seem to be many of us, considering the millions that have almost left her; but then we must remember that twelve, only twelve, conquered the world.

In faith and in hope and in love we must continue to protect the Church, to build it up. But how can we do it? By loving one another, and showing it. By humility, by weakness, by poverty, by living the Beatitudes. This is the only way we can protect the Church; there is no other way. In a word, we must live the Gospel without compromise. That is the Church's protection: that we really be Christians.

When I say we must protect the Church I simply mean that we must affirm, with every sinew of our body, the words of Christ: "Without Me you can do nothing."

Night and day, pounding into my heart are the words, "This is the hour." You see, we have already lost the working man in many places of the world, and we are certainly not welcome in mission fields these days. Right now we don't even know if we can stay in our missions.

But all this is bigger than everything I am talking about. The Church which Christ founded through his incarnation, death and resurrection will live forever; there is no question about that. But have you the right, as a priest, to send the Church into the catacombs, as so many of you seem to be doing right now?

For me to write these things to you is to show you a love that is beyond any explanation. There are no words in my vocabulary to tell you how much I love you. I cannot explain

the unexplainable. I cannot even understand myself, but all
the time, beating against my ears like a tom-tom I hear, "This
is the time, this is the time. It matters not that you are a
woman, that you belong to an unimportant little apostolate. It
matters not. Speak out. Tell them."

Tell them what? What can I tell you? Incoherent words,
fragments of ideas that come and go in my mind, my heart and
soul. But, you see, good, bad or indifferent, God has appointed
me. I must speak because the Church is in danger, grave danger. That is to say, its members are in grave danger of being
alienated from God, and that is the greatest sin. There is no
other. To fall out of love with God is the greatest sin.

Your role is to tell us how to pray, how to love, how to
hope. Your role is to show us the tenderness of Christ, his compassion, and his mercy. This is what will protect the Church.
This is what will bring about its rebirth. Nothing else will. Not
your learning, nor your genius. No, they do not affect it. Only
God's truth as it comes through you, after you yourself have
agonized over it, prayed over it, gone into the darkness of faith
and come out with joy. That will teach us, that will protect the
Church; and that alone.

This is the hour for the healing of the Church, and it is you
who have to lay your hands upon us, the laity, and on each
other, and allow the Holy Spirit to enter. We must forget so
many things that the centuries have crammed into our heads
and we must return to the Man who was in a hurry and who
walked across a little country like Palestine preaching that the
kingdom of God is in our midst.

Do the same. Go around preaching it in that strange weakness which is the essence of all holiness. "I glory in my weakness," says St. Paul. But please do it soon, because the Church
is in terrible danger from within. The danger is the lack of love
of its members for one another.

The hour for prayer and fasting is at hand. The healing of the Church, which also means the healing of ourselves, lies in fasting and prayer. They will lead us to love. Love will lead us to compassion and tenderness and mercy.

Like Christ, blown by the wind of the Holy Spirit, you will crisscross the world like a pilgrim. Wherever you are, in your room or in a monastery or parish, your heart will be wide open to everybody and you will take in the whole world, as a shepherd must. You will know that you are a priest to the Hindu, a priest to the Jew, a priest to Christians, and a priest to every human being in this world.

The kingdom of love shall indeed flourish among us if you show us how to love one another, how to forgive our enemies, and how to lay down our life for the other. Give us Christ instead of yourself!

The hour is very close. There is so little time!

X | Anointed teachers

"A priest understands all things, a priest forgives all things, a priest encompasses all things."

Not long ago several priests and nuns who had just finished two years of studying pastoral theology visited Madonna House. We were sitting around a large table on a dock overlooking our beautiful Madawaska River. They were explaining (interrupting each other politely from time to time) all about their course. They were a bit excited about it; yet at the same time there was something in their voices that held a question mark. It was as though having drunk of all this knowledge, they found it lacking in something that they could not define.

I was puzzled because just before they came I had been praying Psalm 23, *The Lord is my Shepherd*. The word "shepherd" is the same as the word "pastor" but our modern times are not very familiar with shepherds. A pastor is one who shepherds sheep; who takes his flock out to pasture. It all seemed rather simple to me, an everyday affair that Christ seemed to love so much that he mentioned it many times in his Gospels.

If you went through the Gospels with the word pastor in mind, or shepherd, this whole matter of pastoral theology would be lying in the hollow of your hand. "The Lord is my Shepherd, I lack nothing." It seemed to me that these good, holy religious had first to understand that they lack nothing. They should know that they are *anawim*, poor ones who have nothing, and hence are totally dependent upon God. That seemed to be the essence of pastoral theology.

When the priest, the pastor, the shepherd, understands this, he will be transformed. Perhaps he will even enter the transformation of Jesus Christ on Mount Tabor! Once a priest knows who he is—that of himself he is nothing; he is totally dependent upon God—his voice changes. It becomes filled with tenderness, compassion and love. The sheep hear this and follow wherever he leads. In the East, as most everyone knows, the shepherd walks ahead, and the sheep follow.

The psalm says: "In meadows of green grass he lets me lie. To the waters of repose he leads me; there he revives my soul." While my visitors were talking with that strange, little question mark in their voices, I thought that God had indeed to bring the shepherds, the pastors, to the green grass, to the waters of repose to revive their soul. Before any priest can really go and find his flock in order to lead it to God, he has to incarnate this "pastoral theology."

In thinking of the priesthood I sometimes imagined priests as skeletons whose bones have been covered with God's own incarnated flesh: the flesh of Jesus Christ. I thought again of the great and eternal mystery of God becoming man, and then transforming men into himself.

I thought of how he leads priests to the green meadows of this mystery and lets them lie there. Men who lie in the green meadows of the Lord are not too concerned about what is going to happen to them. They are immersed, engulfed, absorbed in a total faith and utter trust and confidence in him. Pastoral theology seems far removed from all this, like some kind of whisper that one had heard somewhere.

How long do those priests lie in his meadows? How long does he let them drink of the waters of his repose that revive their souls? No one can tell, for this is the moment when a priest truly becomes pastor and shepherd. Now he is totally concerned about his flock and his sheep, not about himself. Once this has been achieved, the priest is ready to "enter" the flock! Now is the time of entry.

Before this he walked ahead, as walk he should, and the flock followed him. But now his skeleton is covered and filled with Christ (as it will be again and again) and the zeal of the priest, the pastor, the shepherd, flares up like a flame. There may be black sheep out there; some may be lost in the brambles; some might be threatened by wolves. There are many things that a priest has to do besides lead the sheep to pasture. But it seemed to me that, while my friends were still talking about pastoral theology, a priest wouldn't be able to do very much, or anything, if he thinks that he can do it all by himself. Without God no one can do anything.

The psalm goes on: "He guides me by paths of virtue for the sake of his name." So here is the priest, the pastor, the shepherd, moving now within the flock. What else is he doing? He preaches even while he is finding the black sheep, or extricating those in the brambles. He preaches the Good News to the poor. All of the flock is poor. By preaching the Good News he guides his flock by "the path of virtue." This is what my holy guests were telling me while discussing this "pastoral theology" they had studied.

I wondered why people spend such a long time learning what is so very obvious. In my heart and soul I could not connect this situation with something so official, so seemingly structured as "pastoral theology." My heart connected it with love, for all of this had something to do with love. Christ said that a shepherd is a lover of his flock, or he isn't a shepherd but a hireling. Christ said that unless a man loved his flock, he was a hireling. The hireling never dies for his flock. The shepherd, a lover, does.

Well, priests, pastors, shepherds, obviously are lovers. And they are supposed to guide me and everybody else, by the "path of virtue for his name's sake." So what is any priest doing among the people of God, among his flock? He is teaching virtue. Why is he doing that? The answer is self-evident in the psalm. He is doing it for the sake of Jesus Christ. He is not a hireling; he is a lover, a lover who makes straight the paths of the Lord for his flock, for he knows that he has to lead them by the straight and narrow path: the one that Jesus trod.

"Though I pass through a gloomy valley I fear no harm; beside me your rod and staff are there to hearten me." The pastor, the shepherd, the priest is in the midst of his flock leading them directly to the Father through the Son "in virtue." And virtue, of course, is the law of love.

So the priest, the pastor, the shepherd, is preaching the Good News to his flock in order to bring each one of them into the arms of the Father through Jesus Christ. Now the mystery deepens, because the flock is you and I, men, women, and children. Now the mystery of persons, and the mystery of God blend in the priest. The man who is a lover has been truly filled with Christ, by Christ, for Christ, and we can clearly see the Trinity enter the flock through the pastor. "Yahweh is my Shepherd." But Yahweh, Jesus Christ, and the Spirit are one. It is a mystery we cannot separate. He truly is my shepherd, which is why I lack nothing.

The Holy Trinity is in the priest, pastor, shepherd in a very special way. He brings this Trinity to every member of his flock. Each one of us has the Father, the Son, and the Holy Spirit in his heart from baptism. Yes, the priest, the pastor, the shepherd, makes us walk a very narrow path up the mountain of the Lord, where, at every turn, things become clearer to us. God's pastor, his shepherd, is leading us to the summit of God's mountain where he, we, and the Triune will be one.

"Make straight the path of the Lord," says God to the priest, the pastor, the shepherd. I am a path; you are a path.

Now, by the grace of the Lord and with the help of the shepherd, I am able to lift my weak hands and begin to build within myself—with pick, shovel, or whatever—a straight path to the Lord, for I, too, belong to a priestly people and a kingly people.

"You prepare a table before me under the eyes of my enemies; you anoint my head with oil, my cup brims over." The good, holy religious were still talking, and I was still listening, when I realized that indeed the shepherd was helping me to make a straight path to the Lord within my own soul, and that he was doing it by offering the Holy Eucharist in the midst of his flock of which I am a part. The Lord is not only a shepherd. He is also a host. He lays his beautiful table in the midst of the flock. It is his priest who can transform the bread and wine upon that table into God himself, to give to all of us baptized in the name of the Father, Son and Holy Spirit—food for the journey that we, the flock, must take.

God loves us so much that the food is himself, his priest bringing it forth, for he alone has the power and the glory of transforming bread and wine into God's Body and Blood—our Food.

Now with the shepherd and the flock fed with God, where are the foes that would dare to attack?

The guests stopped talking. I became aware that we all were living in the house of God, wherever we were. And once more, dimly yet clearly, (for in the Spirit these things can happen at the same time), I understood what pastoral theology was all about. It was really a question of hirelings and lovers.

I realized that the best preparation for it was prayer, the prayer of the Eucharist, the prayer of the Bible, the prayer of silence. Somehow, quite unconsciously, we had all become silent. The question marks having died, our silence became deep and intimate. The Good Shepherd was among us, attending us—priests, nuns and myself. It was an almost perfect moment. All of us had suddenly and totally forgotten all about pastoral theology, because we had met the pastor.

Christ wants priests to feed his lambs the maximum, not the minimum. They have often been fed with pap and so do not grow into maturity.

Christ made himself wine and bread, but theologians have given the little ones stones to eat. When persons are fed stones instead of bread, their hearts become hard; people's hearts petrify without the truth.

People are divided, bewildered, misled, unable to find their way in the maze presented to them. Christ's words are taken out from icy caves in the hearts of the men who have a living coal upon their lips. The crowds are given water from a tepid well, while Christ's heady wine is hidden in their cellars. The unencompassable Lord is hemmed in with walls erected of words that have no meat.

We must not give place to the abstract thoughts that man delights in, in presenting his God. For we have become complex—we, the teachers, delighting in the sound of our own voices. The One who is everywhere, whose face no one can see and live, can be found by following, in the dust, red drops from his head. The multitudes have nothing to eat. Why give them stones when you can give the cry of a Child, the feel of a garment, and red drops in the dust? Give them the Christ of Palestine.

The teachers have been caught in complexity, for they were afraid of simplicity. Their mind was awake, but their hearts asleep. Their words turned to straw caught by the wind. Anointed teachers, let the oil that anointed you seep through your will. Put your feet in the footsteps of Christ's naked feet.

Do not seek words that mean so little. You know Christ's words; do not make them into cheap words that compromise his meaning. Be direct and very simple, a worthy herald of the Word, one who stands ready to be lifted up with him. People's hearts are cold; the grace of God is a flame waiting for the priest to speak.

Christ sends a liquid flame upon the earth. It cleanses all it touches. He pours this liquid fire within the hearts of priests. Yet they are afraid, because where Christ is, there is the shadow of the sign of their salvation. Your weakness is your strength, when you are humble and your heart is loving.

You are called to be a beacon in darkness. Be watchful that your light is not dimmed, for there are so few who show the way. See that the Source of Light is not cut off. Speak as those who burn with love alone can speak. Speaking truth, of course, may well push one deeper into the bottomless abyss of Christ's pain!

Christ needs priests who have suffered; priests who are ready to go, taking neither gold nor silver; priests who will bring love back upon earth. Did you think that you could bring his love to all the hungry, with hands that are not pierced? Or that still hold some particle of self? The Paraclete has come to cleanse and empty you. Accept Christ's gifts of pain. You have been chosen: you are ordinary weak men, but strong in Him.

Pray for courage! For fear can make fools of the wisest men. Perfect love casts out all fears, and pain becomes but joy.

The harvest is white, and the laborers are asleep. How can the hearts of priests sleep? Followers of the Crucified, *alter Christus*, look at your hands. Don't you feel the imprint of the nails? Isn't your heart pierced with a lance? Or have you allowed the scabs of comfort and ease to erase the wounds of love? This kind of sleep is exorcised only by prayer, fasting and penance.

If he hesitates, a priest has only to remember that two sets of footprints run side by side, when he follows those of Christ, for Our Lady walks beside him. Power and protection come with invoking her name.

Think of Mary's courage as she goes on visitation to her cousin Elizabeth where two miracles meet: virginal pregnancy and senile pregnancy. In this is a mystery for priests. In their ever-renewed youth, virginal and carrying Christ, they go over hill and dale, figuratively speaking, in search of those whose souls are sterile and old. They bring Christ to them and make them fruitful and rejoicing.

If you are past your youth and feel that the dreams you had before ordination are now wrapped up and laid away on a shelf, go to Mary. She will unwrap them and ask her Spouse to let his power and strength flow through you anew.

Ordinariness is God's gift to men. Each priest must discover what ordinariness holds for him. As the grain of wheat dies, the harvest is already ripening. Faithfulness in little things atones for shriveled souls that worship only self, and yet belong to God.

The heart of the world is cold and complacent, but Christ's heart is fire and flame that can warm the death-bed into life. Priests are called to be the bellows that enkindle responding sparks in the hearts of men.

The world is sick, sick with the leprosy of sin, the wounds of doubt, minds that know no peace, the lameness of divided hearts, cancerous growths of hate. No remedies will help except complete surrender, tears of compunction, and faces prostrated in the dust before God the Father.

Why are the flocks of the Lord so mediocre, fearful, and unkempt? Why is the salt losing its savour? Why is the leaven not lifting up the bread? The mighty and the great are waxing fat and pompous, and forgetting that they are the servants of the flock. Urgency should drive you in your zeal.

O servants of servants, start washing people's feet. Go to them, enter their loneliness and pain. Make it yours, as Christ made your pain his.

The touch of the Mother of God gives priests the power to enter hearts as she does, to heal and restore, repair and clear away debris. Her gentleness is filled with power. Mary is protection; more terrible than an army arrayed for battle. She comes also as an eternal refugee and walks with those in flight.

The winds of hell and heaven clash and fight within men's hearts. Titanic is the battle; yet the wind of love will conquer in the end. You must push back the wind of hate with the strong wind of love.

Where is the poverty of priests? Where is the burning hunger for Christ and the all-consuming love of him? What bellows can fan this fire?

Christ is a priest without vestments, nailed naked to a cross. Yet the hearts of some shepherds do not want to be moved from the valleys of comforts. They do not want to go up the hillsides to where the sheep are dying. They have gathered them into some corral quite close, where they won't have to bestir their limbs. The food, the Church's teaching, is meagre there, and the waters are muddy, not like those on the green hills of the Lord which were created for pastures. The shepherds wear blinders of complacency so as not to look at the vision that can be seen from the summit of the Lord's hill.

Be on guard against not wanting to have much to do with the poor, and being quick to call someone else to attend to them. He who divorces the poor from God loses his God. The heritage of each poor man is a royal dignity, because the poor are Christ in a special way.

When touched and contaminated by the leprosy of greed and comfort, of a thousand needs that are not needs but illusions, priests waste their time, for they should be serving Christ who dwells in the poor.

If you yourself are poor, the Lord will pour through you such wealth as will make paupers of all the rich ones of the earth. Poverty is the key to there being born in your heart new insights, new plans and dreams.

Yes, the world is sick, but take hope. The Mother of God comes swiftly and shapes and forms the hearts of priests. The leprosy of sin yields to her touch, and hate vanishes, and doubts change into faith, and divided hearts become whole again. Life surges anew as in springtime.

Christ has called you priests, chosen as he once chose his small band, called you to go forth into the night, into the storms, into the pack of wolves, to bring his light, his love, his breath, his strength to the flock who follow you and to those who have strayed into the thorns. Bring them back! It is Christ's passionate desire that you bring them back to his heart.

We laity are Christ's pebbles, to be placed in his slingshot to conquer the Goliaths of our time—or to be made into a rampart for the Church. The voice of little pebbles rolling in with the waves will be heard across the noise of machines, across the noise within people's hearts, across all that makes them forget. We may be ridiculed, persecuted and despised, but Mary, Our Lady of the Trinity, will unite those who turn to her and use them to confound the strong.

Christ's folly is the folly of the Cross. His folly is taking roots in the hearts of many. Somewhere, priests speak of love and are willing to plant his Cross in humble places. In the midst of darkness and violence, a gentle stream of light can be seen. It will swell into a sea or a mighty river. The sea is surging; be not afraid. It will multiply the fishes; they will flow in silver streams.

Christ is the cornerstone of a house built on himself. He makes all things new. He makes the desert bloom. He will again be a cornerstone where now there are ruins. Each priest must walk in his darkness with eyes wide open to see the light. Tears wash off the blindness of priests.

To find Christ, a priest has only to take one step inward. He is there, closer to you than your heartbeats, closer than each of your breaths. He lets himself be contained by you; and he contains you. You exist in him. You do not make a step that is outside of his all-encompassing love, that is outside of himself.

Stand still, interiorly, for Christ is where you perhaps seek him not: in your own soul. Ask the Holy Spirit to keep you on your journey inward. The Holy Spirit descended on the little conclave in the Upper Room; he, the Spirit of God, is spouse of Mary. She will lead you to the peace you need. Realize that mystery dwells within your midst, and mystery is pain and joy. Her hands are filled with grace. Her face bends over you. She helps you begin again.

The dignity of priests must be based on charity, simplicity and humility, that reflect Christ's love. Priestly dignity comes from the mantle of the Poor Man of Galilee, which he places on them. The mantle was woven by Mary.

XI

A new vision of priesthood

"A priest is a man whose goal is to be another Christ; a priest is a man who lives to serve."

The following meditation by Catherine Doherty was presented by her as an ordination gift to the first Madonna House staff worker called to the Sacrament of Priesthood, on May 31, 1963. She imagined herself as if she were that man, who had been a convert to the Church and a layman in the Madonna House family, and was now called to the priesthood.

To understand this meditation one should know that Catherine was convinced that a radical change must take place in the way priests are prepared for this holy sacrament. She does not advocate a new "priest-worker" movement. She is not disdainful of the studies which every priest must take on. But she cries out from her deepest heart that the priest understand and embrace a radical and deep humility from which he will be able to see the priesthood with the eyes of Christ.

It was her dream that such priests would be prepared by living a hidden life of poverty, chastity and obedience in a loving, Gospel community—first as a humble, working layman and then as priest.

We are well aware that few of you will have had such a preparation but we include an edited form of her message in the hope that priests will discover a new sense of the humility we need in order to be priests and not clerics; of the hiddenness we need in order to be

servants and not masters; and of the love we need in order to be
Christ's priests and not our own.

Lord, I am about to become your priest. Forgive me if I cannot
yet encompass this truth. For I am a human creature, a man of
infinite poverty, having nothing of my own; even my next
breath lies in the hollow of your hand.

Yet I am about to become your priest. How can my soul
span the heights, the depths, the splendour of this truth? How
can it do so, and remain within my house of sod?

I know that my infinite poverty is going to be clothed in
the incredible holiness and beauty of your priesthood. That
your power will flow through my whole being. That through
me, a poor man, the Divine Pauper and the Eternal Priest will
offer the Eternal Sacrifice to the Father and change ordinary
bread and wine into your own Body and Blood, which I will be
able to give to the multitudes at your Eucharistic banquet. I
will behold the spendthriftness of your love for all persons,
whom you desire to feed with your own flesh so that they and
you may become one.

I know that you will pardon sins through me, that those
whose sins I forgive in your name will be forgiven, and that
those whose sins I bind, shall be bound. Power to heal will be
mine, for you desire to heal through me.

Incomprehensibly I feel myself transparent, emerging,
flowing into you, for indeed you draw me—draw me not only
after yourself (that you did years ago), but now you draw me
into yourself so that already it seems that I am not, but you are!

I know that I shall have to walk the steep, long road to
Calvary. I know that I will have to strip myself and nail myself
to the other side of your cross and be lifted up with you, before
what I feel today will really come to pass. Only then will I be
able to say truthfully what every priest must say at the end of

his life, if he wants to be the priest you want him to be: "I live not, Christ liveth in me."

Yes, Lord, I am about to become a priest, your priest. But I shall become a very unique priest, because I am the first priest to be ordained for Madonna House. There has been no one so ordained before me.

Madonna House is small. It is a simple, little Lay Apostolate, as yet not too popular with many who matter and with many who don't. It is a strange place, a sign of contradiction to many. Why have you led me to it? I have to be truthful with you, Lord: this questions haunts me.

You answer nothing, Lord. Yet I hear the music of your silence, which sings in my soul. Suddenly it seems to me that time has ceased to exist for me, and that I hear your voice clearly, coming from somewhere in a strange land, in an Upper Room. I see you rising from Supper, laying your garments aside, taking a towel and washing the feet of your apostles. I see Peter resisting before giving in.

Then it is all over, and you are putting your garments on again and sitting down at the head of the table. Now your voice comes clearly to me, "Do you understand what it is that I have done to you? You hail me as Master and Lord, and you are right. That is what I am. Therefore if I have washed your feet, I who am Master and Lord, you must also wash one another's feet. I have been setting you an example which will teach you to do what I have done for you."

Now all that has vanished and I am back at Madonna House, knowing why you led me here: you want me to be servant of all, even unto the washing of feet, not only of other priests, but of all the faithful. For these you have ordained me. I hear your voice saying, "I have come to serve."

Yes, you want to teach me that a priest is the servant of all, even unto the washing, not only of unclean souls—which you alone can do, through me as your instrument—but also unto

the washing of feet, which means rendering any kind of service to my brethren that I as a man and a priest can give them.

You want to restore your true image in the mind and soul
and heart of each person, and the image is so simple. It is the
image of a working man, of a carpenter with calloused hands
and a strong body. It is the image of the Lord and Master of the
universe, the Creator, who has made himself not only a man, a
human being, but a servant to all, even unto washing men's
feet.

You tell me that nothing is too menial, too simple, too
small or humble for me to be concerned about, or to do. I can
see myself working on a farm with my anointed hands, not
soiled but cleansed by the contact with Mother Earth.

I begin to realize that when I do this she, Mother Earth,
will give me much material for meditation. For this Mother
Earth of ours will remind me that I am "dust and unto dust I
shall return." Yes, there will be infinite material for meditation
as I weed and hoe and plant, if that should be my duty of the
moment according to your will.

At times I will be amongst my brethren carrying heavy
burdens, unloading trucks or loading them, with gifts given for
the poor. While doing so, I know that you will open my mind,
heart and soul to the burdens, actual burdens, of humanity.
How many of my brothers and sisters—even children—in
many parts of the world carry heavy loads of stone, sand, water,
sugar cane, or bananas, on their heads and shoulders. All of
these will pass before me, through your grace and your teachings, while I heave heavy cartons of clothing and large pieces
of furniture from basement to truck and from truck to basement.

Yes, you want me to understand and to feel in my very
bones, sinews, and the muscles of my back and arms, the
weight of the cross that you carried, and that so much of
humanity has to carry.

I can foresee that when I go the missions I will not only have to make my bed and sweep my room, but maybe make the bed and sweep the room of many a poor man. As my vision is enlarging I thank you, Lord, for having touched my eyes with the spittle of your grace, for you are bringing me back to Nazareth, to your own home, where probably you often did these things for Joseph and Mary.

Yes, I begin to understand "Why Madonna House?" For it will lead me into the humility and sanctity of your hidden years, there to study without any books—and I think mostly from Mary—the way you, my Lord and Creator, lived as a man for so many years. I begin to see that I must dwell in Nazareth, learning there the lesson of how to become the servant of all.

In listening to your silence I dwell on that simple piece of bread and that cup of wine that stands before me on the altar table at Mass, and which, through your power and yet through me, will become in a moment your Flesh and your Blood which I will eat and drink, and so will all those who come to my Mass.

You love us so much that you want to be "eaten up" by us. You give yourself as food and drink to us. What does it mean to be a priest? It means that I must be "eaten up." It means that I must be always available to everyone, to anyone who stands in need of me, your priest.

As I think of that word availability, I feel tired already. Forgive me, Lord, for I am human and weak. It is not easy to be eaten up. I know that my emotions, my human nature, will seek a thousand excuses. A million escapes will appear to me at the time to be sensible and, above all, logical.

Give me the grace to see clearly that all of those excuses are but a whisper of Satan, and to remember the words you said to St. Paul: "My grace is sufficient." May I not only remember these words, but live by them and incarnate them into every second, minute and hour of my priestly day.

I know that when exhausted under the weight of my burdens I will fall on the road, but that you will be there to lift me up. At the same time you will allow me to taste the dust of which I am made, even as you who made it had to taste it on the way to Calvary. Yes, I must allow myself to be eaten up by being always available. I, too, must become a spendthrift of love, of strength, and of power even as you have been.

The music of your silence continues. My soul hears it. My heart thanks you for it and my mind rejoices in it. With the psalmist I, too, want to sing: "O God, you are my God for whom I long; for you my flesh pines, and my soul thirsts like the earth, parched and lifeless without water. How I love your law, O Lord! It is my meditation all day."

I begin to understand that I must arise and go and seek you out. I must make your law, your beauty, your perfection seen by all so that, like your wounds, they may touch them in me. How am I to do this, Lord? The answer comes to me that, as always, I must seek it in my neighbour, for there I shall find you.

As I meditate, suddenly I feel the cold of a dark night touch me. The sun seems to be blotted out, and I am filled with fears and doubts. For I begin to understand that yours is the Law of Love, and the only way to show it to others, as show it I must because I am another you, is to show them the wounds of my crucifixion.

That means, inescapably, that I must crucify myself. This comes to me with such strength and force that I seem to have entered the darkest of nights. Fear is walking with me, for I am weak, O Lord, I am weak.

I know that I must pray in this night for the gift of faith, of a constantly growing faith which will help me love. It will bring me your love, which will enlarge my heart and set it on fire so that I shall become a light enkindled by the flame of your Holy Spirit, a light to my neighbour's feet.

Yes, I must be crucified, for I must show your wounds to everyone. To be crucified I must have faith. Then I will know you who are love, and you will be my strength. "Lord, I believe. Help my unbelief!"

As a priest, a servant of all, whom you have chosen to cry your Gospel in the market place as you have cried it, I will have to preach (and then you will be preaching) in the churches and chapels to which you will bring me. But I will have to preach it also in log cabins and bamboo huts, on country roads and city streets, eating, walking, working, sleeping, just living. I must preach it by my very life and with every breath I take. The Gospel must be written again, not on papyrus or parchments, but on and in my priestly life. For this you have ordained me.

You have been good to me, Lord. You have given me another unwritten book to learn from. For though I am the first priest to be ordained for Madonna House, you have brought other priests to it who were already ordained, even before I received the precious gift of faith.

It is from their lives, their sufferings, their adaptations to the lay apostolate that I have learned much. Because they are humble men, reticent men, they will not tell me at once what I have to learn, but I must find out. Help me to do so. Teach me to sit at their feet, a humble beggar, asking for the precious knowledge that they have to give me. For they have walked the paths I shall have to walk.

They have persevered through sweat and blood, suffering and pain, that now are hidden from me. Speak to them, Lord, and tell them how small and weak I am, and why they should reveal the hidden beauty of their vocation to me, a young priest. For I must learn now, at the beginning, the true price priests have to pay for souls.

A priest must be willing and ready to be crucified on the other side of your cross, to be lifted up in the market place so as to show your wounds to all who pass by. He must be available to everyone, everywhere, at all times. He must be the servant of all. He must live in Nazareth as a carpenter, a workman. There he must learn that the Lord of Hosts did not consider menial work lowering or degrading, for he did it for many years. Neither must I.

A priest must learn to bear the burdens and share the work of his lay brothers and sisters in serving and restoring others in Christ.

A priest must show your priesthood to the world, must live it as you lived it on earth in its pristine purity. Your people have somehow forgotten you, because your priestly face is smeared and disfigured by the pomp and outward wealth of the Church.

I see that I must be poor as you were poor, with a deep poverty of utter obedience to the Father's will. But I must also be poor in worldly goods and in comforts.

Let me never forget that poverty will penetrate deeply, that Lady Poverty will show me that her wealth lies in little things done exceedingly well for love of you, and for your glory and that of the Father. I know that you will lead me through humble, ordinary paths, the paths of little things—the paths in Nazareth that you walked over and over again for more than thirty years.

The music of your silence grows fainter, Lord. The thought that I am about to become your priest grows stronger, and though I cannot yet encompass this truth—I don't think I ever will be able to encompass it until I see you face to face—nevertheless, Beloved, my soul is at peace. I stand ready, with your grace, to be clothed in a few days with the incredible holiness and beauty of your Priesthood.

Now there is silence in my soul also. All that I can offer you, Lord, at this moment, is the song of my loving and grateful silence. All words have left me, and only my silence humbly attempts to answer your loving silence. Alleluia! Alleluia! Alleluia!

XII | A life offered for priests

"A priest is a man who has crucified himself so that he too may be lifted up and draw all things to Christ."

Catherine de Hueck Doherty was no maudlin, religious romantic. With one arm always stretched out to God and the other to every neighbour, she had both feet on the ground. Her life unfolded in a long, painful fiat and ended with a mysterious alleluia. Gradually we in Madonna House are beginning to realize what a giant of faith she was, a mystic in every sense of the word. Now the official title "Servant of God" may be used, signifying that the cause for her canonization may proceed.

In 1953 Catherine heard the Lord ask her to become a victim soul for bishops and priests and to uphold the Holy Father. It was to be her "second vocation." Through it she loved priests—those who knew of her love personally as well as thousands who did not—with a most unusual passion.

These few meager paragraphs from her diary give ample evidence not only of the cost of that victimhood but its ultimate joy to her and its lesson to us.

Let us not be afraid to ask her intercession so that we, too, may become a new sign of Christ's love for our people in spite of our human weaknesses.

She began this dairy at the age of 21, in 1918.

January 1, 1918:

The new year began. Bless it my Lord! Bring calm to my poor martyred country [Russia, then in the throes of revolution] and to me with Beloved Borinka [a Russian form of the name, Boris, her husband's name]. Bless us with your grace.

Overview, 1924–1937:

In this period Catherine went from rags to riches, and back to rags again. She took odd jobs in New York City to support her family. Then came unexpected popularity and world travel as a lecture agent, followed by the disintegration of her marriage. These years also saw the glorious birth and tragic death of her Friendship House in Toronto and the total defamation of her character.

February 8, 1927:

My God, if I did not have faith in your infinite mercy I would not try to reform myself, for my path is one failure after another. Jesus, what a spiritual failure I am. As I write this in the quiet chapel of the Cenacle before your altar I feel like running away, so clearly do I see myself, my sins, my utter failure, my nothingness. Yet I love you, and I cannot go, for I know my place is here before you always. I cannot forget you, even in the midst of the uproarious noise of the world's good time. I think of you and seem to hear your voice.

My Jesus, why do you delight in showering graces upon one so utterly unworthy as I? Is it because my very inconsistency and absolute unfitness calls the Good Shepherd? It must be. Oh Jesus, I love you! Help me, dear Lord, to show you in deeds that I love you!

Give me humility, poverty of spirit, perseverance. What a mockery, my dear Lord, is my life. What a success I am in material life—and what a failure otherwise. But you will not abandon me. You will help me over the rough parts of the road, my Jesus, won't you? I know you will, for you have promised to do so. There is nothing but you: the Truth, the Way, the Life! I love, love, love you. Teach me to love you more and more. O my Beloved! Forgive me.

February 8, 1930:

A restlessness possesses me. I know it so well. Its origin is perhaps hidden in physical and biological reasons but its effects are far-reaching. Oh, what do I care where it all comes from? My blood is on fire. I want love and passion. I want the sweetness of the kiss of the one who loves me, wants me. Oh Lord, help. I have but to stretch out my hands and my desire will be fulfilled and yet, as before, I must not. You who have given me strength before, help me. I am alone in the face of temptation.

May 26, 1934:

"What does it profit a man to gain this whole world and lose his soul." (Mt 16:26)

My Jesus, give me the grace to understand. Make me realize very fully that the world has nothing to offer me. That I am here only to do thy will, which is my eternal salvation. Jesus! Give me the grace to see it. Also, give me the grace to do it, to occupy myself with my eternal salvation primarily.

Please Jesus, I have loved you all my life, but look at that life: up and down. Promises given to you, only to be broken. Sanctification started, only to be stopped. Times of close union with you, broken for the friendship, so ephemeral, of men! Sins of omission, sins of commission. What graces have you not showered on me! And I have passed them by, not cooperated with them.

And now you knock again. Give me ears that hear your knock, eyes that see your hand in all my life, brains or intelli-

gence to grasp the meaning of the invitation, and strength to
go and do your command.

Is it possible that you can forgive badly prepared and made
confessions; cold, almost blasphemous communions?
Ambitions, so hidden from the eyes of men.

Is it possible that I can still be forgiven, O Jesus? Son of
Man, great is your mercy. Blessed be thou, O Lord, for the
grace, the privilege of this retreat. Also for the realization of
the goal of my life: my eternal salvation.

30 June 1934:

Dear Jesus, I am so tired today, so terribly tired. All I want
to do is sleep. There is no desire in me to get up to go to
church, to communion. My heart is heavy within me.
Yesterday evening, prayers were like a stone around my neck.
Forgive me, Jesus, I will try again. The only thing that keeps
me to my rule is will.

Somehow my thoughts are muddled today. O Jesus, help
me.

Overview, 1938–1965:
*Catherine went to Europe on assignment with the Catholic maga-
zine,* The Sign, *and picked up the first hints of another world war.
She moved to Harlem in New York and began another Friendship
House, this time with African Americans. She met Eddie Doherty,
the flamboyant Chicago newspaper writer, and they were married in
1942 after her first marriage was annulled. In 1947 they came to
Combermere, Ontario, Canada, and gave birth to Madonna
House.*

18 January 1938:

How beautiful Mass is! At times one can almost feel the presence of our Lord, and after Communion there is such love, awe, and sense of the infinite in one's heart that it seems impossible that so many people don't know him or, what is worse, knowing about him, do not believe in him. The pity of it! Great desire comes into my heart to go forth and tell them about him, make them love him at all cost.

Then, dark and forbidding, the cost rises before me: misunderstandings, persecution by one's own, stripping of all things men value, even honour (for a woman doubly hard), each step wrought with suffering, sacrifice and pain. I know it from personal experience and yet, when after Communion I go back deep down within myself and adore the God within me, nothing seems to matter. Only he, and the stupendous love he bore us.

24 May 1938:

Beloved, how really beautiful are thy tabernacles, those of souls! As I journey forth on my pilgrimage from one human shrine to another, I stand breathless before the beauty of human souls. O Christ compassionate, you have built well! But how close I come to despair when I see thy temples desecrated, my Beloved Holy Ghost! And what darkness engulfs me when I see that the desecration is so often due to the shattering of that intangible, yet precious dream we call "ideals".

Lord, I pray for thy priests. They have lost that inner sight which is theirs by your grace. O Jesus, you see the tragedy of these souls far better than my sinful eyes can see; you see the revolt of the laity against the darkness or lack of fitness of the clergy.

You see how they struggle before their broken ideal; the violation of thy laws by a person especially consecrated to observe them. Powerless, I pray for them and beg you to hear my poor sinful prayer. I will add a way of the cross daily for them, Beloved. And offer my Mass intention daily for them. Hear my cry, give holiness to thy priests.

13 October 1938:

Beloved, how wonderful you are, how close. How I love your priests, for your reflected glory shines in their faces. Their hands hold our God. Holy men: miracles of God, of love and grace. How tragic is the anti-clericalism which is raising its head daily in the world. It is as if men today took pleasure in tearing apart our Father's house, brick by brick, stone by stone. St. Francis, you whom Christ bid to repair his house, help us to see and to love and repair, not destroy it!

Overview, 1966–1985:

These years mark the on-going purification of a whole new lay apostolate; ordained and unordained men and women live together in peace and love, pax *and* caritas. *Catherine died in 1985.*

March 5, 1966:

Lord, you know my tiredness, for you truly know my sitting and my standing up. You know all about me. I am tired because your Church is heavy on my heart. You have placed into my heart a passionate love of you, the Church, people...

Loving you, I want, oh so terribly much, to bring you to all, and all to you! And yet there is but one way to do it and that is by emptying myself of myself: *kenosis!* So that you truly can pass through me to others.

When I behold my poverty and sinfulness—I am so slow to empty myself of myself—I weep, as I weep over the world! But then as I weep I realize, oh so clearly, that I depend on you and you alone, on your love and mercy, and I am strangely consoled and at peace.

Yet I pray you teach me to be more empty. Teach me to love with your heart, more and more. I must bring your, our, children to you. These you entrusted to me. Help me. My love for them grows like a sea—and they do not swim in its warm waters. The sea and warm water stand as symbols for peace, happiness, and justice.

Sometimes their despair burns like a consuming fire which I cannot endure, or so it seems; then I fall, inwardly, like one dead. Yet if I am in public, I speak, work, answer, dictate letters. I do not know how this can be, but it is!

I fall under the weight of humanity and its hunger. Suddenly, Christ rises in me and in humanity. Is this illusion? Whatever it is, it is real to me and the Christ in me kisses, embraces the Christ in or from humanity! At this moment joy, peace, serenity—an indescribable state of affairs—fill me. Then all of it vanishes, as if it were not.

April 27, 1974:

Yesterday the doctor reported the result of my X-ray. Degeneration of my spine was the verdict, and with it, of course, pain everywhere. My feet and my hands are as if they were asleep, especially at night. Also arthritis is prevalent in my hands; very painful! In fact, it is already at times unbearable. It is good that I am alone, for again and again I cry out because of pain, in the hands and knees especially.

To cry out in the night! You did, Beloved, in Gethsemane. Almost like you, I want to serve, not to be served.

The Lord has his ways and he has taught me again and again his desires. It seems to me that now he is teaching me his ways deeply and profoundly. Pain is the kiss of Christ...

Now I think I shall know deeper pain than ever before. Physical pain and mental, too. I know, Lord, I shall be weak, frightened, and it may happen that I will wish to turn my face away from your lips! Please, please do not let this happen, dear One. Please instead give me courage to face all you want me to face. Kiss me again and again, Lord. I love you!

I realize that all these symptoms are a sort of preparation for my death. Alleluia! But give me the courage to bear the symptoms. Also I wish, deeply wish, to offer all my pains for the Apostolate, so that the members be yours!

10 September 1977:

A strange lassitude takes hold of me these days. All things seem to be removed from me as if I am outdistancing them. Alone God comes closer, ever closer.

There are times when I seem to attend Mass—and yet attend is not the word. I am part of it, united to God in the strangest incomprehensible way! But then it is always thus these days. Yes it is. God possesses me utterly. I am lost in him, totally, or so it seems. Always he is on my mind, and yet it is not my mind that he is in. No, he is in my heart. I love him passionately in my own fashion, inexplicable even to me.

The interior state of "void" is always near these days, always. It seems as if God has given me the key to its door! I feel so remote from all people and things and yet I am closer to all of them than I ever have been before. It is as if I can encompass them most easily—and in total detachment, yet attachment. Truly it is all a great mystery to me. All I know is that I desire but what God desires.

XIII | Our Lady, mother of the priesthood

*"Mary is my life. I hope that I never have any other...
She will lead me to her Son."*

No book by Catherine Doherty or about her can be complete without some comment on her intense relationship with the Mother of God. In the same way no book about priests or to them would be complete without a specific focus on Our Lady, mother of the priesthood.

When people said to Catherine, "You don't often speak of Mary," she would look amazed, even hurt. And then very gently say something like, "Speak of her? I speak to her all day everyday. I live with her in Nazareth. This house is named after her— Madonna House. Her images are everywhere. She is at the center of our life of faith. She helps me bake the bread and write the letters. She is my mother and the mother of my Lord. I am consecrated to her. I don't need to speak of her. Mary is my life!"

Those aren't her words exactly but they express both the shock and the intensity of Catherine's response. And, as with other subjects in her life, it would take books to do justice to her sense of the presence and the place of the Mother of God in her life and in the life of the Church, to do justice to her unique Marian theology.

As priests, we must always re-examine our Marian theology and the everyday reality of the Mother of God in our lives and in our ministry. Given the stature of Catherine Doherty as an outspoken evangelist of the Church's social-gospel teachings in the 20's,

30's and 40's and as a world-renowned foundress of a very unique
family in that Church it might sound strange to hear her say:

> "On the Feast of Our Lady's Purification, February 2, 1951,
> I finished a long journey...My journey ended at the feet of Our
> Lady's altar, in the church of the Sacred Heart in Ottawa,
> Canada, where my husband, Eddie Doherty, and I consecrat-
> ed ourselves to her...We consecrated ourselves to her entirely
> and forever. The long journey was ended. Or had it only
> begun?"

My brothers, here is a woman whose words of intense and heroic faith we have just read from her own diary beginning in 1918 and
yet she is not ashamed to tell us that this specific consecration to the
Mother of God was a focal point in her whole life. We should think
about that, those of us who have a "problem" with the Mother of
God in our personal lives or our parish ministry, or for whom she is
little more than a "May Devotion." Listen to some of Catherine's
own words about this Blessed Mother.

Before I could speak any language properly, when I was just a
little child, I knew Mary. Her icon, or painted image, hung in
my parents' bedroom. It was ancient and dark with time, but
sparkling with family gems embedded in it as offerings of peti-
tions and gratitude. A *lampada* or vigil light always burned
before it, except on Good Friday.

My parents called her *Bogoroditza*, meaning "She who gave
birth to God." But to me she was just Mary our Mother. When
my parents went out in the evening they would bring me, all
warm and cozy and half asleep, to her icon and pray that she
take care of me while they were gone.

If I was naughty it was not enough for me to apologize to
Mother and Father, or whomever else I had to apologize to. Off

I was sent to apologize to Mary. She would present my apologies to her divine Son, as He would accept them more readily from her hands. This was, of course, beyond me at the time, and I just said, "Sorry, Mother Mary." But as time went on, I understood how right that was.

If there was a special joy in our house—a great feast day, trip, vacation, or one's namesday (in Russia these are celebrated in preference to birthdays), or any kind of good fortune, one shared it with Our Lady by leaving some candles or a new toy on the little table before her icon, where Mother always kept some flowers or plants. Mary would offer these joys to her divine Son. For joys, sorrows, pain, repentance—everything in life came to us, her earthly children, from him, through her hands—and they were to be given back to him through her, as gifts of our love.

Even gifts and anything nice that we liked had to be shared with her Son, through her. He and his Mother would then give these things to poor children. For unless we shared all things with God and his gracious mother, through the poor, how could we ever hope to see them after death? Hadn't Christ said, "Whatsoever you do to the least of my brothers you do to me"? It was never too early to start that sharing.

Thus slowly, naturally, imperceptibly, Mary, the Mother of God, entered my life and permeated it. She was there when I awoke, as I gave my day to her for her Son. She was there when I went to school. It was good to know that she was close. She was there in our children's games. She brought her Son to play with us, or so it seemed.

Later it was quite clear that she watched us. There were moments in our youth when my brothers or I would like to hide from her motherly eye and grasp this or that forbidden fruit, but she was always there—in the comforting security of deep, deep faith. Mary, Mother of sinners, was close and would help me to pick myself up.

Years passed, and tragedy came into my life, seemingly without end. I entered the immense domain of Lady Pain through war and the atheistic communist revolution that came to me, mine, and Holy Russia.

Then Our Lady came into her own in my life. Because I knew her, because from babyhood my life had been lived within her radiant shadow, because my feet had followed her through every Joyful Mystery of the rosary, it was only natural that I turned to her when the Sorrowful Mysteries of our faith came into my life.

Gethsemane became a reality for me. I saw my loved ones led one by one to slaughter: arrested, imprisoned unjustly, executed summarily, while I myself lived under the exhausting mental suffering of waiting for the same fate to overtake me. Finally the blow fell, and I knew imprisonment and clearly saw the face of death.

I was condemned to die by hunger, which reduced my body to weakness and blanketed my mind with terror, and God receded until it seemed he was not there, and I was lying in the dust of endless converging roads leading to despair. Is it any wonder that Our Mother came then, and, taking me by the hand, walked once more the Way of the Cross, this time with me and with thousands of my compatriots, as she had done with her own Son?

Half delirious from hunger, weakness, and mental pain, I repeated, like a refrain, one word: Mary, Mary, Mary. Her name and her person brought light into my stygian darkness. She kept me from going over the thin, icy, cold edge of despair. Her name was benediction and oil to my wounds. It was more, for in her—the gate to the Way that is Christ; the daughter of the Father, in whom he is well pleased; the spouse of the Holy Spirit, the crimson dove of Love—lies the secret of Uncreated Light, the secret of our hope, in hopelessness.

She, the shelter of the shelterless, the "House of Gold," opened the door to me and allowed me to enter and to understand that no one is tried beyond their capacity. She, the mediatrix of all graces, will bring graces enough, and more, to every Christian. Thus we are enabled to say that *fiat* which each of us must say before the mystery of the Cross when it is our turn to lie on it and be nailed to it.

The Mother of Joy brought joy into my desert of pain and death. She showed me the way to Love Incarnate, her Son, and made my Calvary acceptable, even infinitely desirable, through his. She brought the radiance of his peace to shine on me in the midst of Satan's un-peace.

She took my spirit into her blessed hands, and just as, when I was a child, my own mother used to lift me up for our heavenly Mother's nightly blessing, so now Mary lifted me up for the blessing of the Father, Son, and Holy Spirit. Or so it seemed to my exhausted mind and body, into which flowed a new and strong life of faith and hope and love.

Years later, when all these dark days of earthly hell were but a memory, I understood that she who had walked with me to all my schools and experiences, had finally taken me into her own school of holy silence and love.

On the Feast of Our Lady's Purification, February 2, 1951, I finished a long journey. My journey ended at the feet of Our Lady's altar, in the church of the Sacred Heart in Ottawa, Canada, where my husband, Eddie Doherty, and I consecrated ourselves to her. We consecrated ourselves to her entirely and forever. One long journey was ended. Another began.

Mary is my life. I hope I never have any other, for my life is passed under the finely wrought posts of her gate. Some day the gate will open, and she will lead me to her Son. In the meantime I shall wait at the posts of her gate, seeking to mold my life ever more unto hers, dwelling in her holy silence and motherly love.

We Russians always thought of her in two terms: as an ordinary young girl who was a teenager when she became pregnant, and as a mature woman, strong enough to stand silent and surrendering under the cross of her Son.

There is a legend which says that two learned rabbis were discussing the Scriptures about the coming messiah, when a humble young woman from Nazareth made obeisance to them as she passed by. It was Mary; and they scarcely noticed her. That happens to us, too, sometimes.

Mary is the very fabric of our lives. Her *fiat* to God's plan is ours, and we know that she said *fiat* not just once, but thousands of times. We know this instinctively, because she believed, even when she didn't understand. "Let it be done to me according to your Word."

When she became pregnant, there would have been a great shame attached, because she and Joseph were not yet married, only betrothed; and he was going to put her away. But never once did she open her mouth to justify herself. Now, she was not Christ before Pilate. She was an ordinary girl from a village. Dear Fathers, doesn't that give us courage to be silent before unjust accusations? She didn't think it out theologically; she's so simple.

Yes, we always thought of her in realistic terms. She got up in the morning, and on some days of the week carried the laundry to the pool. The women of Nazareth must have come to her constantly because she was who she was. She must have kept, not a cookie jar, but the Eastern sweets that Eastern people love, and children must have come to her.

We also think of her as the woman with the power to stand silently under the cross of her Son, and who in some incredible way, realized at that moment that she was chosen to be the mother of all the men and women for whom he had died.

She's the woman of speech and the woman of silence. She's stronger than an army in battle array and as weak as only

a woman can be, with God. Her life was a sea of small things—
so insignificantly small that they're almost not worth men-
tioning. The corn had to be ground, her house swept, meals
prepared, cloth woven. Day after day the Mother of God did
those things.

Dear Fathers, from her we can learn the quality of listening, of taking human words as well as God's words, and hold-
ing them in our hearts until the Holy Spirit cracks them open
and gives their inner meaning to us as he did to her.

Our Lady is just as much a part of our life as breathing. If I
stop taking air in and letting it out, I die. That's the way it is
with our relationship to the Mother of God, too.

If you don't know her, you will never know her Son,
because the immense mystery of our faith is that God chose
this ordinary village girl for his mother. Jesus lived with her for
a time after Joseph died. He was the breadwinner; he made
chairs and tables; he was a man. And then one day, without
saying much to her, he went away—and a strange mystery
began. Together with the other holy women, she evidently followed him, but she still had the house in Nazareth.

One day when she went to see him, the people said, "Your
mother is outside." He replied, "Who is my mother?" She must
have made another *fiat* then, perhaps without understanding.
What was it like, being the mother of this strange man, day in
and day out, in the surroundings she was brought up in and
lived in—the culture, the religion of an obedient daughter of
Israel?

She was there when he was flagellated and she followed
him in his passion. We have no record that she wept or that
she spoke. We only know that she went to live with John the
Beloved.

After Christ' death the eleven frightened apostles went
into an upper room and stayed there as he told them. Mary was
there too, and she seemed to be the mainstay of those men

who, only the day before, perhaps didn't notice her when she was following her Son with the other three women.

Who is Our Lady? She is someone who is with me as a friend, someone with whom I can talk, and who has me in her heart. Who else has lived with God as Mary has? From whom can we better learn to know the Incarnate One than from the woman who carried him for nine months in her womb? We should all talk to her about her Son.

Beloved Fathers, don't forget to put into our hands the slender thread of Our Lady's Psalter, now known as the rosary. It can hold our tragic world above the abyss that yawns below it, and may yet, with your help, lift it from its present dark depths.

How can anyone talk about throwing out devotions to Our Lady? Do we want to throw out the woman who was pregnant with God and who will lead us always to him?

If one thinks of her mainly as Queen of Angels or Queen of the Universe, then it is not astonishing that one would not know her. For Christ our God was a carpenter and Mary a housewife; yet Christ, in heaven, still has calloused hands in his glorified body—and his mother who has been assumed into heaven also has a glorified body, with hands that show she was a working woman.

Here we are catching sight of a mystery encased in human flesh, born from a human mother and a human father, Joachim and Anne. Mary has been given to us by Christ as our mother, and now that she is in heaven she has the secret of everything. When you are worried about something or have a difficulty in spiritual matters, why not go to her?

---

* Much of this chapter is adapted from Catherine's book, *Bogoroditza: She Who Gave Birth to God.* (Combermere: Madonna House Publications, 2001)

Prayer for Catherine's Intercession

All loving Father, through your beloved Son, Jesus, we have been taught to ask for what we need. And through his spouse, our Mother the Church, we have been instructed to pray for one another, and to ask the intercession of your servants, who have fallen asleep in Christ. Therefore, through the intercession of your servant, Catherine Doherty, we ask

[that our priestly lives will be a constant fiat to your will].

We ask this for your honour and glory, and in the name of Jesus Christ, your Son Our Lord. Amen.

For private use only.
Imprimatur: ✝ *J.R. Windle, Bishop of Pembroke, May 1, 1993.*

About the Author

Catherine de Hueck Doherty

Catherine Kolyschkine was born into a wealthy family in Russia on the feast of the Assumption, August 15, 1896 (N.S.). She was baptized in the Russian Orthodox Church, although many Christian strands were woven into the spiritual fabric of her family, including Catholicism. During her father's long assignments abroad in connection with Russian diplomatic and business interests, Catherine was entrusted to convent schools and Catholic nuns. However, the distinctively Russian incarnation of the Gospel was the great crucible into which every other element poured to forge Catherine's early life.

From the liturgy of the Russian Orthodox Church, the living faith of her father and mother, and the earthy piety of the Russian people themselves, sinners and skeptics as well as saints, she received the powerful spiritual traditions and symbols of the Christian East.

At fifteen Catherine was married to Boris de Hueck. Soon they were swept into the devastating battles of World War I, she as a nurse, he as an engineer. After the Revolution of 1917, they endured with all the peoples of the Russian Empire the agonies of starvation and civil war. Many of Catherine's relatives were killed, but she and Boris escaped at last and, stripped of everything but clothes and faith, made their way to Finland and then to England.

It was in England that Catherine formally became a Catholic. At the beginning of her new life in the West, Catherine accepted the teachings of the Catholic Church, without rejecting, then or ever, the spiritual wealth of her Orthodox heritage.

In 1921, Boris and Catherine, with little money and uncertain health, sailed to Canada. She was pregnant and gave birth to their son, George, soon after they arrived in their new country. They settled in Toronto, but even with the help of friends it was not easy to find work that would support them and their child. Catherine often remembered that she had first come to know the people of North America not through wealthy benefactors who were intrigued by her aristocratic connections, but in the working poor whose lives she shared as maid, laundress, waitress and salesclerk.

Soon Catherine's intelligence, energy, and gift for public speaking brought her to the attention of a large lecture bureau. Her talks were popular all across Canada and the United States. Within a few years, she became an executive with another, international lecture service. Before long she had a large apartment, many books, a nurse for her son, a fine car, celebrated friends. She was a North American success story.

But Catherine began to wonder. Her marriage was disintegrating, and she seemed unable to heal it. Moreover, she knew that she was also struggling with God. Had he saved her from death in Russia so many times only to make her a comfortable bourgeoise in North America?

The words of Christ haunted her: "Sell all you possess, and give it to the poor, and come, follow me." It seemed madness, and she tried to close her soul to these words, which she has described as sounding within her like the faint, disjointed stammering of a dying man. She could not escape them.

In the early 1930s, after several years of anguish, Catherine and Boris separated permanently; later, the Church annulled their marriage. As devastated as Catherine was by what felt to her yet another, more intimate death, she knew that God wanted something new from her now. But she did not know what it was.

It was to the Archbishop of Toronto, Neil McNeil, that she turned for help in her need for a word from the Lord. The Archbishop listened to Catherine and told her that he believed God was asking something most unusual from her, something that would demand her own crucifixion on the other side of the cross of Christ. Did she love Christ enough to do that?

Catherine did. She agreed to spend a year in prayer for further discernment, and when the year was over, the Archbishop gave Catherine his blessing, and she and her son went to live in a humble section of the city. George was enrolled in a good school, and Catherine began to seek to obey the Lord's word to her "to become one with the poor, one with him."

At first Catherine desired only to be with the poor, to love and serve them very quietly, to become their friend, to pray with them, hidden in their midst. But when others saw her and heard her speak, they wanted to join her. There was an intensity to her faith and love that lit a flame in the hearts of many men and women. Catherine had not envisaged a community, but when the Archbishop told her that, yes, Christ was calling her to found a community of lay people to serve him in the poor, she accepted what he said. Soon Friendship House was born.

The works of Friendship House were modest—a shelter for the homeless, meals for the hungry, recreation and books for the young, a newspaper to make known the social teachings of the Church. The prophetic voice of Catherine and the community of Friendship House resounded boldly, however, in a city where Catholics were not well accepted. The poor welcomed her, but others were scandalized by her forceful insistence that caring for the poor was not optional for Christians. After a few years, misunderstanding and gossip drove her out of Toronto. The first Friendship House was dead.

Yet Catherine's voice had reached other ears in North America. In 1938 Father John LaFarge, S.J., arranged to have the Archbishop of New York invite her to work in Harlem. She agreed to start Friendship House again, alone, in total poverty, this time among the African–Americans. Catherine brought them not only compassion and an irresistible passion for justice, but her whole soul.

Once again men and women came to share her life and work. The interracial apostolate grew in New York and expanded to other cities, to Chicago, Washington, D.C., and Portland, Oregon. Friendship House became well known, if not necessarily well thought of, in the American Church. Catherine shared with her friend Dorothy Day of the Catholic Worker, the intense struggle to move the gospel out of books into believers' lives. Even if a few, such as the young Thomas Merton, recognized in her the power of the Holy Spirit and an unwavering fidelity to Christ's Church, many others were frightened by her Russian bluntness. Others simply could not grasp the largeness of her vision, especially because her experience of the ways of God were so foreign to them. Finally after a painful difference of opinion over the nature of the Friendship House apostolate, Catherine found herself pushed again into the chartless waters of the Lord.

This time, however, Catherine did not have to start alone. In 1943, she had married Eddie Doherty, a celebrated newspaperman, after he convinced her and her bishop that he wanted to share and support her vocation. In 1947, then, Catherine and Eddie came to Combermere, a small village 180 miles northeast of Toronto, where the Bishop of Pembroke had agreed she could work among the rural families.

They came bewildered and uncertain. Still exhausted with grief of another separation, they planted a dozen apple trees. Somehow they knew that they had come home, and that the mysterious vocation of prayer, communal love and simple service of the poor, which the Lord had given to Catherine, would not be lost. They could not see what the future held, and often during the first years in Combermere they were tempted to leave. But they had planted those trees, and if they had come to what seemed to them a wilderness, they knew that it was the Lord's and that he would make it bloom.

He did. Again others came to join Catherine, and this time priests came to stay as well. The apostolate, now called Madonna House, grew slowly. Father John T. Callahan, the founder–director of the priests of Madonna House, was a constant support.

In 1955, when the community had agreed to establish itself more formally in the Church with vows of poverty, chastity and obedience leading to a life–time commitment, Catherine and Eddie took a vow of celibacy. Their sacrifice bore fruit in vocations and in stability, and in 1978 Bishop Joseph R. Windle approved the constitution of Madonna House as a single community with branches of laymen, lay-women and clerics. (Under the new code of canon law, the apostolate is a public association of the faithful.)

At present, over fifty years later, Madonna House has more than 200 members, including twenty priests, along with a number of applicants and 132 associate priests. The apostolate has missions in Belgium, Brazil, France, England, Ghana, Liberia, and Russia, in addition to fourteen others in Canada and the United States. The training center in Combermere offers an experience of the gospel life to hundreds every year.

As Catherine's inner life deepened and the community matured, she was better able to share with us the fullness of the inner vocation Christ had formed in her through the many blessings and struggles of her life. "Love is ingenious", she liked to say, and the ingenuity of her heart and her mind found new words and deeds to show us how deep and how broad was the call Madonna House had received through her "to restore all things in Christ."

FATHER ROBERT PELTON
Madonna House Apostolate

More information about Catherine Doherty's life, works, and news about the progress of her cause for canonization can be found at the Internet web site: **www.catherinedoherty.org**

Also by Catherine Doherty

Madonna House Classics:

Poustinia: Encountering God in Silence, Solitude and Prayer
Sobornost: Experiencing Unity of Mind, Heart and Soul
Strannik: The Call to the Pilgrimage of the Heart
Molchanie: Experiencing The Silence of God
Uródivoi: Fools for God
Bogoroditza: She Who Gave Birth to God

Apostolic Farming: Healing the Earth
Dearly Beloved: Letters to the Children of My Spirit
Dear Parents: A Gift of Love for Families
Dear Seminarian
Donkey Bells: Advent and Christmas
Doubts, Loneliness, Rejection
Fragments of My Life: A Memoir
Grace in Every Season: Through the Year with Catherine Doherty
The Gospel of a Poor Woman
The Gospel Without Compromise
Journey Inward: Interior Conversations
Kiss of Christ: Experiencing Healing Forgiveness through Confession
Listening For The Call: Embracing Your Vocation
Lubov: The Heart of the Beloved
Moments of Grace desk calendar
My Heart And I: Spiritual Reflections
My Russian Yesterdays
Not Without Parables: Stories of Yesterday, Today and Eternity
O Jesus: Prayers from the Diaries of Catherine Doherty
Season of Mercy: Lent and Easter
Soul of My Soul: Reflections From a Life of Prayer
Welcome, Pilgrim

Audio Talks:

Catherine Doherty Talks to Families
Giving Your Life to God: A Retreat
Love One Another: A Talk on Living the Gospel

Available from Madonna House Publications: 1-888-703-7110

An essential resource for both priests and laity:

CATHERINE DOHERTY'S MADONNA HOUSE CLASSICS SERIES

POUSTINIA
Encountering God in Silence, Solitude and Prayer

The modern spiritual classic for those seeking the open heart and listening soul of a silent contemplation. *Poustinia*, a Russian word, means "desert", a place to meet Christ in silence, solitude and prayer. Men and women who desire communion with God can discover how the poustinia powerfully fulfills their yearning. Readers are invited to leave the noise and harried pace of daily life to enter a place of silence and solitude. (Now also available on cassette in AudioBook format.)

Paperback ISBN 0-921440-54-5   AudioBook ISBN 0-921440-53-7

SOBORNOST
Experiencing Unity of Mind, Heart and Soul

Discover how your heart can be softened and opened to the transforming reality of the Holy Trinity dwelling within you. In *Sobornost*, the Russian word for "unity," Catherine leads her readers on the journey of a lifetime. She guides us along the pathway that takes us home to God's house, into the graced intimacy of eternal belonging. Here we rediscover the final unity that flows from Divine Persons, one in love—Father, Son, and Spirit. (Now also available on cassette in AudioBook format.)

Paperback ISBN 0-921440-25-1   AudioBook ISBN 0-921440-57-X

STRANNIK
The Call to the Pilgrimage of the Heart

Learn how to fulfill the hunger and dream of the pilgrimage that we must all take to unity with God. *Strannik* is Russian for "pilgrim", one with a vocation—a unique, holy calling. Catherine shows that pilgrimage is not just something for a few spiritual ascetics with wanderlust. The true strannik begins by looking within the self, where God already is.

Paperback ISBN 0-921440-24-3   AudioBook ISBN 0-921440-77-4

Molchanie
Experiencing the Silence of God

In language poetic and meditative yet direct and simple, Catherine invites us to share her own pilgrimage into God's silence. Pilgrimage lasts as long as one's life, and involves purification, union with God, work and suffering, culminating in the almost miraculous experience of the divine silence. Much of *Molchanie* is in the way of allegory, full of visions and imagination—it is an allegorical pilgrimage.

Paperback ISBN 0-921440-28-6

Uródivoi
Holy Fools

Learn why humility is the foundation of the spiritual journey, and how to become one forever with the humble, glorified Christ. *Uródivoi* is a Russian word meaning "holy foolishness", and in this book, inspired by her Russian upbringing and the words of St. Paul, Catherine expresses her calling to this aspect of Russian spirituality, and calls us to become fools for Christ.

Paperback ISBN 0-921440-34-0

Bogoroditza
She Who Gave Birth to God

In *Bogoroditza*, Catherine Doherty speaks of how in the midst of many poignant life experiences she turned to Our Lady for help. A book for every person who needs the strong, tender love of the Mother who is always with us, caring for us, revealing her Son to us.

Paperback ISBN 0-921440-48-0

The entire six-volume Madonna House Classics Series is also available at a special price in one complete set. Please call for details.

Order Toll Free: 1-888-703-7110

MADONNA HOUSE PUBLICATIONS
COMBERMERE • ONTARIO • CANADA • K0J 1L0

Madonna House Publications is a non-profit apostolate, faithful to the teachings of the Catholic Church.

"Lord, give bread to the hungry and hunger for You to those who have bread," was a favourite prayer of our foundress, Catherine Doherty. At Madonna House Publications, we strive to satisfy both of these fundamental needs.

Through our books, we aim to feed the spiritual hunger for God in our readers with the words of the Gospel and to awaken and deepen in them an experience of Jesus' love in the most simple and ordinary facets of everyday life.

Any proceeds—and donations from friends like you—allow us to assist missionaries with books for people who cannot afford them but most need them, all around the world.

May God bless you for your participation in this apostolate!

To request a catalogue of our current publications, please call (613) 756-3728, or write to us at:

Madonna House Publications
2888 Dafoe Rd
Combermere ON   K0J 1L0
Canada

You can also visit us on the Internet at the following address:

www.madonnahouse.org/publications